D1527798

THE WONDER OF THE REAL

To

Sister Mary of the
Sacred Heart

on her Silver
jubilee
April 27, 1973

With Love

Fr. Frank

THE WONDER OF
THE REAL

A Sketch in Basic Philosophy

By

FRANCIS J. KLAUDER, S.D.B., Ph.D.

THE CHRISTOPHER PUBLISHING HOUSE
NORTH QUINCY, MASS. 02171

Nihil Obstat: Joseph M. Occhio, S.D.B., S.T.L., Ph.D.
Censor Librorum
Imprimi Potest: John J. Malloy, S.D.B., S.T.L., M.A.
Provincial
† Imprimatur: Lawrence B. Casey, D.D.
Bishop of Paterson
December 8, 1972

PRINTED IN

THE UNITED STATES OF AMERICA

TO
HARRY W. RASMUSSEN

*. . . scire omnia venire a Deo, et semper
ad Deum ascendere per medium quod est
Christus, Verbum incarnatum . . . et sic
eris verus metaphysicus.*

CONTENTS

Contents

LIST OF ILLUSTRATIONS

11

INTRODUCTION

The question that the human mind never tires of asking is: "Why?" "Why?" It is the query made about a thousand things. Man wants to know the reasons for everyday occurrences, for the laws of nature, for the origin of the world. And why not?

The purpose of Science is to arrange and coordinate the answers to man's manifold questions in every field of knowledge. From this vast human effort there results the impressive array of distinct sciences, or coordinated systems of knowledge through causes, which modern ingenuity seems to multiply with succeeding generations. No need to try listing them all. Suffice it to say that, in attempting to discover the "why" of things in the various areas of knowledge, some sciences are concerned with "know-how" rather than with the theoretical knowledge of what things are. This provides the most general division of the sciences into the practical and speculative.

Again, in seeking the causes of things, speculative science can stop at the proximate reasons (those closest at hand); or it can delve into the deepest mysteries of existence and human life. If the former, we have the physical and mathematical sciences. If the latter, we are in the realm of *philosophy,* which is the science of all things in their ultimate causes, as far as the human intellect can gauge.

Philosophy, therefore, differs from the other sciences. It has a much wider scope than they do. Each of the physical or mathematical sciences concentrates its attention on a particular portion of reality and seeks to understand its chosen realm in tangible, sensible or measurable terms. Such sciences rely heavily on the senses and on scientific instruments. Instead, philosophy passes beyond these boundaries, seeking by the light of the intellect to pierce beneath the sensible aspects of reality and reach their purely intelligible and supra-sensible foundations, as far as these present themselves to human view. From this venture there result the speculative parts of philosophy, which is usually divided into General Metaphysics, Cosmology, Rational Psychology and the Philosophy of God.

The Meaning of Metaphysics

The present work is limited to sketching the first and most fundamental part of philosophy—General Metaphysics. It is called "Metaphysics" because it deals with what is beyond the physical or sensible, the prefix "meta" meaning "beyond" in Greek. It is called "General" because it seeks the ultimate explanations of *all* reality whether infrahuman, human or divine. And it seeks the elements that are *common* to all things from the very fact that they are. It is, therefore, defined as the Science of being *as being.* Indeed, other sciences all study reality or "being"; but only General Metaphysics studies the common elements and principles governing *being as such,* being of any sort, being of all kinds.

Obviously, such a science is very important, since it formulates knowledge which all other sciences take for granted. At this point, it is necessary to assert that this sketch in basic philosophy approaches its subject matter from the so-called *realistic* point of view. We hold it a fact, in the first place, that there is reality, and that the human intellect is capable of knowing it, and that this is the very purpose of philosophy itself. Not all philosophers treat the matter in this way, as for example, the Idealists, who say that ideas are the only reality. Defending the "realistic" position, understood in this sense, is the task of a special branch of philosophy, which is called Epistemology. Epistemology serves as a good introduction to Metaphysics, but it lies beyond the scope of the present work.

Division of the Work

In this work we will first consider the meaning of the real; then we will consider the various kinds of reality, the distinction between the "One" and the "many," the interrelationships of all things, the goodness, truth and otherness, which characterizes all things, and finally the whole and entire ensemble of this wondrous world.

1.

THE REAL

"All philosophy begins in wonder." These words of Aristotle seem to apply to all philosophers, but not in the same way. Some philosophers have wondered over the material universe. Others were impressed with the world of spirit. Still others have been puzzled with the fact of change. They have begun their philosophies accordingly, and their initial attitude is reflected from the beginning to the end of their philosophies.

The philosophy of Aristotle and St. Thomas Aquinas (and Scholastic Philosophy in general) begins with *wonder over the real.* The thing that we all take for granted —the existence of reality itself—is the most amazing wonder of all. To be or not to be—that is the question! Why is there something rather than nothing? What does it mean *to be*?

Reality—or being—is, then, the prized subject matter of our philosophical investigation in our present work. We are immediately faced with a difficulty, for people do not ordinarily get excited over "being." It is so commonplace! It is found everywhere. We are unable to think without positing it in our minds. It saturates all things.

"However," writes Jacques Maritain, "we must remember that the best way of hiding anything is to make it common, to place it among the most ordinary objects. We all thus understand that the being of metaphysics, the highest and most hidden thing in the natural order, is concealed in the being of common sense. Nothing is more ordinary than being, if we mean the being of everyday knowledge; nothing more hidden if we mean the being of Metaphysics. . . .It is by reason of its pure simplicity, because it is too simple, almost superhumanly simple, that it eludes philosophers who have not risen to the necessary degree of abstraction and visualization. . . .It is from the most ordinary common knowledge that the metaphysician educes it, draws it out of its ironical commonplace to look it full in the face." Jacques Maritain, *A Preface to Metaphysics* (N.Y., Mentor Omega Books, 1962), pp. 87-9.

What Is Being?

The first question we must try to answer is: What is being? What is the real? Webster's dictionary describes being as "that which actually exists." This, indeed, is the primary meaning of being in St. Thomas Aquinas— actual being, or a reality outside the mind and actually existing, independent of the mind. This is *real* being for St. Thomas. But the concept of being can be extended to include possible being, so that a fuller description of being is *"that which is or can be."* However, from the outset we must emphasize that the first meaning of being is something *actual.* Only secondarily does being mean a possible thing. These are the two chief meanings of being.

Another way to describe being is to say that it is something which possesses the perfection of "to be," or existence. We prefer the infinitive form, *to be,* rather than the abstract term, existence, because "to be" is a verb or "action-word" and brings out the dynamic aspect of being. Just as *running* (to run) is the *action* of a runner (or someone running), so "to be" is the *action* par excellence of any being. It is the primary perfection of anything, by which that thing IS. By it, as Maritain puts it, a thing "triumphs over nothingness!" In considering any verb form, such as *run,* we can derive two parts of speech, the noun and the participle, viz. running and runner. *Running* (to run) signifies an action primarily, while implying a subject (someone) doing that action. *Runner* signifies indiscriminately anyone who actually runs or is capable of running. So "being" can be taken in a participial sense as an action (sometimes written be-ing), or as a noun (that which is or can be). As previously indicated, by "being" St. Thomas usually means actual being, that which is (first meaning of the noun), and by "to be" (*esse*) he means the action of be-ing.

How Do We Know Being?

According to Jacques Maritain, the most famous Thomist of the twentieth century, we know being (noun sense) naturally, spontaneously, and necessarily because it is the most basic of all our ideas, which arises in us by the very fact of be-ing or existing. He calls this fundamental human experience—whose beginnings we can hardly trace back in time or memory—*the intuition of being.* It is the basic human experience—the very consciousness of reality itself. It cannot be proven but only recognized for what it is—the matter-of-fact consciousness in a thinker of *reality*. In this act of consciousness, simultaneously we are aware of the distinction between thought and reality, and yet we realize that they are mutually related to each other. (See sketch on page 27.) We recognize reality as something actual, extramental and related to existence; at the same time we understand it as related to our mind and known by it. Therefore, another description of being is an essence (the intelligible structure of a thing capable of being known by the mind) with its relationship to existence. The intuition of being consists, on the one hand, in the recognition of the absolute character of being (its existential, extramental character) and, on the other hand, its simultaneous presence in the mind through its idea. Being is primarily something outside the mind, but it is also a valid idea within the mind. In fact, it is the most fundamental of all ideas, in which and through which our knowledge progresses from the grasp of a few things to many, from vague to clear knowledge, from general to particular kinds of things, and from "being" as universal and common to the distinct understanding of individual instances of being.

Various Kinds of Intuition

In a man's intellectual life there is a triple source of immediate knowledge, whose truth is not proved but is self-evident. Such self-evident or immediate knowledge is called intuition (intuitive).

(a) *Sensible intuition:* An intuition of a concrete object in its *sensible* features. It is the immediate attainment of an exterior object as· "something colored" or "something hard" or the like. In man, however, it is inferior to intelligence, for as such it does not give "truth," which demands judgment.

In the restricted domain of its proper, formal object it is infallible, if everything is in a normal state, in the sense that it expresses the concrete object as it is.

(b) *Intellectual intuition:* This is the immediate attainment of a concrete object as *existing.* This is called the *intuition of being.* Through this intuition, not only is a thing immediately evident, but it is identified with the same object as that of a sensible intuition; and such identification is judged as valid. Thus, the mind is directly placed within the bosom of the exterior world and then returns upon itself through the reflex act of consciousness.

This very reflection itself, according to St. Thomas, constitutes a true intellectual intuition of the thinking self, not in order to know its *essence,* but only its existence. Thus, though the soul must always go through the senses for its intellectual activities, at the same time, in an indirect fashion, it can immediately know itself in its act of thought as an actual and living reality.

(c) *Intuition of common sense:* This intuition yields the first principles which are immediately understood from the richness of being and its transcendental properties of unity, truth and goodness. From this intuitive knowledge, in turn arise (1) the habit of the first principles, (2) synderesis, and (3) the intellectual light for a *scientific* interpretation of the universe. Therefore originating in every man is the basis for Metaphysics, Ethics and the understanding of nature. See Thonnard, *A Short*

History of Philosophy (N.Y., Desclee, 1955), pp. 390-92.

Being as Abstract

Being as found outside the mind is any existing reality. Being as found within the mind—the idea of being—is an abstraction. The case could not be otherwise. Any idea we derive from reality is not the reality itself, but its representation, its re-presence (in a different way) in the mind. So with reality itself—or the idea of reality—it is understood at once as both without and within the mind—in different ways, of course, abstract within the mind, concrete outside the mind. But the abstraction of being is at a deeper level than the abstraction which occurs in the understanding of ordinary things. Material things, as we know them in ordinary experience, present us with varying features in several layers or spheres of knowledge. Thus, for example, in knowing an "apple," I can concentrate my attention on its sensible characteristics; the quantitative relationships between its parts, which are expressible in mathematical terms; or its purely intelligible aspects evident to the intellect alone: first and foremost, its existence (actuality) or being. This is the highest degree of abstraction, not because the object understood is abstract, but because in understanding this feature of the object a person's mind is in the realm of pure intelligence, abstract from sensible and quantitative matter.

The Starting Point of Philosophy

For St. Thomas and his followers, the starting point of philosophy lies in the simple recognition of the actuality of being, not just one's own existence as an actuality but the existence of other things known in the ever-recurring intuition or immediate knowledge of the intellect in and through sensible knowledge. It is a fact raised to the level of philosophical principle. In this recognition the idea of being is accepted as the most simple, the most important and the most far-reaching. It is the most simple idea because there is nothing easier to understand than "to be"—the most fundamental word in any language. It is the most important because all the acts of human knowledge presuppose and employ it. Let us consider the first act of the intellect (i.e., the idea of *anything*), *being* is included. The second act of the mind (i.e., the judgment) consists in affirming or denying a predicate of a subject, e.g., this IS a pencil. The very heart of this judgment, or of any other, is "IS" or some form of that word, expressed or implied. The third act of the intellect (or reasoning) employs ideas and judgments to arrive at new truth—the knowledge of being is presupposed to begin with, and knowledge about being is increased in the process. Being is all-encompassing, transcending all divisions and classifications, applicable to the very differences among the various categories of different things; and for this reason, it is called *transcendental,* i.e., applying to all things, all the divisions or kinds of things, and to the very differences which mark off the varying classes of things.

Quotations From St. Thomas Aquinas

Before concluding this chapter, we wish to include here quotations from the Angelic Doctor from various sources concerning the subject matter on hand. We will present them under three headings: the knowledge of being as natural, the knowledge of being as primary, and the knowledge of being as the source of knowledge.

Knowledge of Being as Natural

1. Our intellect knows being naturally and whatever is *per se* comprised under being as such. *Contra Gentiles,* II, 83.

2. The intellect knows truth by reflecting on itself. *Truth,* I, 9.

3. ...We know principles by simple intuition and without discourse. *Truth,* VIII, 15.

Knowledge of Being as Primary

1. "Being" is the first and most evident thing that the intellect knows, and all other conceptions of the intellect are reducible to this one. *Truth,* I, 1.

2. In the first operation of the mind there is something first which falls under the gaze of the intellect, viz., what I call "BEING." Nor can the mind in its operation understand anything unless "being" is understood. *In Meta.,* IV, 6. See also I *Sent.,* VIII, I, 3.

3. Being is nothing else than *that which is.* It signifies that which first is known by the intellect as an absolute actuality. For "IS," simply speaking, signifies the actuality of be-ing (*in actu esse*). . . .The actuality which is signified by this word "IS" is the actuality that every form has in common, whether that form is substantial or accidental. *Perih.,* I, 5.

Knowledge of Being as the Source of Knowledge

1. For certain seeds of knowledge pre-exist in us,

namely, the first concepts of understanding, which by the light of the agent intellect are immediately known ...as the notions of being, of the one, and so on, which the understanding grasps immediately. In these general principles, however, all the consequences are included as in certain seminal principles. When, therefore, the mind is led from these general notions to actual knowledge of the particular things, which it knew previously in general and, as it were, potentially, then one is said to acquire knowledge. *Truth,* II, 1.

2. All knowledge is in a certain sense implanted in us from the beginning (since we have the light of the agent intellect) through the medium of universal conceptions which are immediately known by the light of the agent intellect. They serve as universal principles through which we judge all things, and in which we foreknow these others. *Truth,* X, 6.

3. In one, who is taught, the knowledge does not exist in complete actuality, but, as it were, in seminal principles, in the sense that the universal concepts which we know naturally are, as it were, the seeds of all knowledge which follows. *Truth,* II, 1 and 5.

Summary

Meaning of being: Being means that which is or can be. It means something with the perfection of be-ing or to be—actuality. Being implies an intelligible essence with its relationship to existence.

Characteristics of the idea of being: most simple, most important and *transcendental.*

Kinds of being: actual and possible being. (A third division is sometimes added—"beings of reason"—to cover such "things" as negations, privations, contradictions, etc., which can exist only in the mind. Our mind is so attuned to "being" that even in trying to understand its opposite, we have to speak in terms of being!)

The intuition of being: the explicit realization that reality is actual. The self, the non-self, and the act of knowledge itself are all understood intuitively (without proof) as actual (being).

St. Thomas Aquinas: being is known as an absolute actuality.

Conclusion: The wonder of the real is that, though being overwhelms us on all sides, it encompasses us, as it were, gently and seems to invite us to explore its ever expanding boundaries.

THE
INTUITION
OF
BEING

2.

LIKE AND UNLIKE

There are many different kinds of reality or being. Not all philosophers have admitted this fact. For St. Thomas, we have here something that cannot be denied, but which needs to be explained. He endeavors to do this by the *analogy of being.*

Simply put, every being is *similar* to every other. Beings are alike inasmuch as they ARE. Yet beings differ from one another in many ways. They are both alike and unlike. This "similarity in difference" constitutes the so-called analogy of being.

If our concept of being is to correspond to the variety that we find in the actual world, we must take this variety into account. Most of our ideas are *univocal* ideas, i.e., they have one meaning, which remains fixed and the same. Take, for example, the concept of MAN. It means a rational animal. The meaning does not admit to degrees, of more or less or of substantial change. But the idea of being is different: it must allow for completely different kinds of beings, because the real world is such a varied one. Being admits of "more or less": a living thing, for example, enjoys a greater degree of being than something nonliving. Being includes substance as well as accident: its meaning can shift from one to the other and still retain its basic reference to "the actual." But because its meaning has shifted some-

what, it is not a univocal concept. And especially, if we
contrast God or the Infinite Being with any finite being,
we see that being cannot be considered univocal. For it
is the very nature of God to exist, which is not the case
for any creature. Or, in the exact words of the Doctor
of the Schools, "God's manner of being is different from
that of any creature, because God IS Being, which can
be said of no creature. Therefore, being is not univocal
when applied to the Creator and to the creature." (*De
Potentia,* VII, 7)

On the other hand, neither can being be called *equivocal,* i.e., a mere word referring to quite different
things, with no connection between them. The word
bark, for example, is an equivocal word—it means different things altogether: the cry (bark) of a dog or the
outer covering (bark) of a tree.

The Meaning of Analogy

An analogy or comparison arises from the similarity
which the mind perceives between two different things.
Such similarity is based on a like characteristic or function enjoyed by both things. For example, the intellect
understands and the eye sees. We can detect a similarity between the function of the eye and the function
of understanding. We can say, by analogy, that the
mind "sees." This analogy is called an analogy of proportionality. In our example, the eye and the intellect
(called "the analogates," or things compared with each
other) share in some perfection, each in its own way.

Let us apply this to beings. Each being exists in its
own way. To each being existence is given according to
its capacity. Since every being shares in possessing its
own existence in a way proper to it, every being is sim-

ilar to each other. It is *similar,* i.e., midway between totally the same and totally different.

The analogy of proportionality is rooted in our everyday experience of the different kinds of things we come in contact with. There is another and deeper analogy or comparison that leads us to a deeper appreciation of being. Such deeper appreciation arises from a further question: "Why are things similar?" How can things be partially alike and partially unlike at the same time? It is a double-edged question which cannot be answered in one breath.

First, let us try to answer *this* question: in our ordinary experience, why do things look alike? Is it not because of some resemblance to their parents? Their similarity is based on their relationship to one whom they imitate. So, in the order of being, all things are similar because they more or less resemble God, Who causes their being and their degree of resemblance to Him. Here we have the "analogy of attribution"—an analogy based on the comparison of several to one, on whom all depend for their being.

There is no end to possible comparisons. That is why "analogy" can become a very intricate topic. But let the above suffice for this "sketch."

Another Meaning of Being

Webster's dictionary gives more than one entry on "being." One of these is "the totality of existing things." If we consider all existing things, as it were, in one community, then their sum total may be called "being." If we take "being" in this sense, we are jointly embracing the two analogies of being: all beings as similar in existing and as dependent on the One Cause, God.

One of the greatest temptations for many philosophers has been pantheism. Spinoza, for example, took being to mean the one substance of God, with which all things are identical. But this is a contradiction. To avoid this, we should remember that all things are *related* to God as effects to Cause; and all things are similar to God and to each other because of their relationship to God. There is a sense, then, in which we can speak of the great family of being, for we can truly say that all things are *relatives* of God. The Sioux Indians expressed a profound thought when they left written: *with all beings we shall be as relatives.* This philosophical truth is often expressed in poetry and art. When understood in an extraordinary intuition, as sometimes happens, it can lead to great joy, as for example in St. Francis of Assisi. But, even if we do not have an intuitive appreciation of the fact, we should try to understand it philosophically; and one way of doing this is through the analogy of being.

There is a great deal to understand in the phrase, "the totality of existing things" or all things and God. The totality of existing things, as we find them, imply God. Without God, they can make no sense. Indeed, an atheistic existentialist, such as Sartre, tells us precisely this. For Sartre, the world is an absurdity.

If we would understand the Whole of reality—or the universe as a Whole—God is necessarily implied as the Transcendent (Superior) Cause and as an Immanent Presence. God reveals Himself through the universe. The sense of God's presence within the universe needs to be re-emphasized today. God and the World—the

World and God—make a Whole, not in a pantheistic sense, but in the sense that the universe apart from God simply cannot exist nor be understood. In other words, the universe is not a Whole without God. God holds the universe together, not as a part of Himself, but as its Beginning, Center and End. When we speak of the *whole universe* we must think primarily of God as its continuing Cause, provident Director and final End.

A correct understanding of being will bring us to this conclusion, at first vaguely, then more clearly, in the immense light of the intellect's own expanding consciousness. In the words of Dulles:

"Being is that to which the mind is naturally akin; for it is always under the aspect of being that the mind grasps its object. Nothing, to be sure, appears in consciousness as *pure being.* That which thrusts itself into our thought is always some particular, determinate being. But in grasping the particular I am aware that it is particular; that it does not exhaustively fulfill the potentialities of being. Thus the mind in knowing transcends itself. Focusing on a particular object present to it, it is obscurely aware of realms beyond. When I seize upon any particular object—such as a chair, for example—that which compels the intellect in the presence of the object is not the fact that it is brown or that it is a chair (I could know it even if it were not a chair or not brown) but the fact that it IS—the absolute value of being. The intellect, then, attains in things that which is opposed only to non-being, to nothingness, to negation. The greatness of human intellect lies, therefore, in the fact that there is nothing completely outside its range. In this sense, it is a transcendental and quasi-infinite faculty." A. Dulles, *Introductory Metaphysics* (N.Y., Sheed and Ward, 1955), pp. 10-11.

The Absoluteness of Being

Since "being" thrusts itself upon us, we can speak of a certain absoluteness of being. We do not mean that any being itself which lies within our immediate experience is absolute. But we mean merely this: the fact that reality exists is something beyond our control. Being imposes itself upon us as an actuality. Therefore, since we do not, and cannot, change this fact, the reality of being lies before us as changeless, unchangeable and eternal in the sense presently to be explained. We are not implying that any being we know directly, or even all reality as it is manifested to us, is positively changeless, unchangeable and eternal. But, in a negative sense, and as far as we are concerned, there is nothing that we can do about the existence of being. Being simply lies beyond our power—past, present and future. In a global sense, we can neither make what has been "not to have been," nor what is not to be, nor what lies in the future not to occur. In this sense, then, being takes on a certain absolute character.

Another Division of Being

We have spoken of the "likeness" or similarity of all things—their resemblances to God. Now we must face the question: what makes things different or unlike? Of course, the full answer to this question will require discussion also in subsequent chapters of this book.

But a very general answer to the question can be given here: there are two general divisions of being because of two contrasting ways of existing. A being that exists independently is called a substance. In this sense, since God exists necessarily, St. John Damascene calls Him the Infinite Ocean of Substance. But the Saint does not understand substance in the same way as Spinoza, for whom God is the only substance. God is the only substance whose existence is absolutely independent of anything outside Himself. There are many things, however, in our experience with a relatively independent existence, viz., animals, trees, other men, etc., but which nevertheless depend upon God and are "in God," but not as parts of Him.

Accidents, unlike substances which can exist in themselves, are properties, characteristics or attributes of substance. They do not naturally exist apart from substance. Aristotle listed nine classes of accidental being (called *predicaments* or *categories*). The most important ones, which all must be studied in Metaphysics, are quantity, quality, relation, action and passion. We will take these up in succeeding chapters.

The distinction between substance and accident is a valid one, although in determining the ultimate stuff of the material universe, it might be difficult to determine whether certain entities are accidental or essential. But living things are certainly substances, as well as any entity which actually exists in itself. The fact of change offers a good proof for the distinction between substance and accident. In an accidental change (e.g., the heating of water) the water (substance) remains, but the temperature (accident) changes. It is a fact also of everyday experience that the human person (an "ego") remains the same substance or subject, while undergoing many accidental changes, viz., weight, increase of knowledge, acquiring of virtue, etc. For Aristotle, the first and primary meaning of being was an independent kind of being, or substance; and accidents are called "being" in relation to their substance. Even today, in fact, it is quite natural, when thinking of being, to think of a substance, i.e., a reality of a substantial kind. For St. Thomas Aquinas, all the substances of the world, together with their accidents, are called being in relation to God, the Infinite Substance. Thus, "being" refers primarily to God as the first substance, then to other substances, then to accidents and finally to all these taken together as forming One Whole, which is not God, but which can neither exist nor be understood without God.

Summary

The Analogy of Being: The meaning of being as partly the same and partly different as applied to various beings. Beings are *similar,* i.e., partly the same and partly different. Therefore, the idea of being applies to its inferiors (all things to which the idea of being applies) in a way partly the same and partly different. Thomists generally distinguish a twofold analogy, which further clarifies the concept. Beings are alike, inasmuch as they share existence according to the capacities of their natures. There is a proportion between their natures (or essences) and their existences. This implies a being whose very nature is to exist and which finite beings more or less resemble. Hence all beings are similar to each other: (1) because they all exist in their own way (analogy of proportionality); (2) because they all refer to, and depend on, One Source, which they imitate (analogy of attribution).

The Absolute Character of Being: While analogy deals with the relative (varying) character of being, there is another aspect which we have called its "absolute" character; being is (negatively) without limit, not within our power to change, implicitly eternal and immense (inasmuch as it is impossible for us to measure it in time or in space.)

The Most General Divisions of Being: The most basic division of being is into substantial being and accidental being. The former is an entity capable of existing on its own. The latter is a perfection apt to exist in another entity and dependent on it. The reality of change, the experience of the individual ego and the very meaning of being itself justifies this distinction.

3.

THE ONE AND THE MANY

How shall we understand the difference between finite and infinite being? This important philosophical
question faces every thinker. In the case of Aristotle,
the answer came in terms of ACT and POTENCY. And
St. Thomas, following Aristotle's lead, formulated this
principle: Act and potency encompass being and every
division of being.

To understand this principle it is necessary first to
grasp the meaning of the terms, *act* and *potency*. Aristotle discovered these concepts in his effort to explain
change. Heraclitus had denied the reality of being in
favor of "becoming" or change; and Parmenides had
rejected change in support of being. Aristotle, in a
matter-of-fact analysis of changing beings, argued as
follows: a thing that has changed has acquired a *perfection* not previously possessed ("act" he called it);
but the thing would not have acquired the perfection
unless it had the *capacity* for it in the first place. He
called the capacity for the perfection *potency*. Change,
therefore, consists in the fact that a thing in potency to
a certain perfection acquires that perfection, under the
influence of a sufficient cause.

Potency, then, is a capacity for a perfection, or "act."
And act is a perfection of any sort. Extending the meaning of these concepts, *act* is any reality in possession of

39

a perfection, e.g., water that is actually hot is "act" in relation to heat. Potency, on the other hand, is any reality which is capable of further perfection, e.g., cold water (capable of being heated).

We have already seen how Aristotle, in explaining accidental change, spoke of "substance" and "accident." Now in terms of potency and act, we may say with Aristotle that substance (in our example, water) is *potency* in relation to heat, which in this context must be considered *act.*

St. Thomas Aquinas took the concepts of act and potency and used them universally. He taught that Reality—being itself—must be understood in terms of act or potency, or both. For, any reality must be considered changeable or unchangeable. If unchangeable, such a being is pure act, i.e., in possession of all perfections—an all perfect being, viz., God. If changeable, a being is act in regard to all the perfections it has, and potency in regard to all the perfections it is capable of. In other words, it is a composite of act and potency. And finally, in considering the fundamental principle of the material universe as something indeterminate, a principle that can take on any and all forms, St. Thomas called it "pure potency" or primary matter. Its corresponding act or acts are the many basic forms of the various kinds of material things known to us. These he called "substantial forms." Matter and form, in this sense, make up the substance or essence of a material thing, which is thus essentially composite of potency and act. This is indicated in the accompanying table, which also introduces us to an important point for our next consideration.

	Act	*Potency*
In the Order of Accidental Perfections	Accident	Substance
In the order of Material Essences	Substantial Form	Primary Matter
In the order of Created Beings	Existence or To Be	Essence

DIVISIONS OF ACT AND POTENCY IN THE
VARIOUS ORDERS OF BEING

Infinite Act

The most important application of potency and act—its application in the realm of all created being—is still to be explained. God alone is Infinite Act, and there cannot be two beings of this sort, for they would be equal or identical to each other. In the order of being, therefore, there is only one unlimited act of existence, which is proper to God alone, the Pure and All-Perfect Being whose nature is TO BE. Every other being must be a composite of potency and act as will be explained.

In the first place, we must point out that act (perfection) of itself does not imply limitation. Therefore, if an act is limited, it must be limited by some principle other than itself, for it would be contradictory for act (perfection) to be the cause of limitation (imperfection). Potency, on the other hand, is an apt principle of limitation, for it denotes *capacity,* so much and no more, for an act. Thus, God, in creating other beings, gives an act of existence according to the capacity of the essence of the thing in question. There is a distinction and proportion in each created thing between its existence and essence as between act and potency. Only in this way can we account for the multiplicity of beings. There is only One Being in which essence equals existence (comparable to the whole number, 1), but in every other being we have a participation in being according to a certain proportion (comparable to a fraction, like ¼, ½, etc., which approaches the integral number, 1, but never can equal it). Thus, the twofold analogy of being is further explained by the real distinction in every creature between essence and existence, related as potency to act.

Importance of the "Real Distinction"

St. Thomas considered this distinction of the utmost importance for understanding the difference between uncreated and created being. He writes:

> ...Every creature may be compared to God, as the air is to the sun which enlightens it. For as the sun possesses light by its nature, and as the air is enlightened by sharing the sun's nature, so God alone is Being by virtue of His own Essence, since His Essence is His existence; whereas every creature has being by participation, so that its essence is not its existence. *Summa,* I, 104, 1.

In more poetic language, St. Augustine expresses the same thought as St. Thomas in the following famous passages:

> "What is God? I asked the earth and it answered: 'It is not I.' Whatever things are in it ut-

tered the same confession. I asked the sea, the
depths, the creeping things among living animals,
and they replied: 'We are not thy God; look above
us.' I asked the airy breezes, and the whole atmos-
phere with its inhabitants said: 'Anaximenes is
mistaken; I am not God.' I asked the sky, the sun,
the moon, the stars: 'Nor are we the God whom
you seek,' they said. And I said to all these things
which surround the entryways of my flesh: 'Tell
me about my God, since you are not He; tell me
something about Him.' With a loud voice, they
cried out: 'He made us.' My interrogation was my
looking upon them, and their reply was their beauty." St. Augustine, *Confessions,* 10, 6.

"I looked closely at the rest of things below Thee
and saw that they are neither wholly in existence,
nor wholly out of existence: they exist, indeed for
they are from Thee, but they do not exist, for they
are not what Thou art. For, that truly is which
endures immutably. Now, it is good for me to
cleave to God, for, if I do not endure in Him, I
cannot in myself. But He endures in Himself and
renews all things, and Thou art my Lord, since
Thou art in no need of my goods." *Ibid.,* 7, 11.

Other Considerations

The distinction between essence and existence in
creatures is important not only to differentiate them
from God, but also to differentiate them among themselves. For all things are alike in the fact of existing.
But there are different *kinds* of beings, according to the
various kinds of essences or natures to which existence

is given. Existence accounts for the universal likeness among things: it cannot simultaneously account for their differences. The fact of difference (among the varying kinds of beings) is explained by a principle distinct from existence, viz., essence. Otherwise, the same principle, i.e., existence, would account for both likeness and difference, which is contradictory.

In his early work, *De Ente et Essentia* (chapter 5), St. Thomas Aquinas also presents the following reasoning for the real distinction between essence and existence in creatures:

> Whatever does not belong to the notion of essence or quiddity comes from without and enters into composition with the essence, for no essence is intelligible without its essential parts. Now, every essence or quiddity can be understood without anything being known of its existing. I can know what a man or a phoenix is and still be ignorant whether it exists in reality. Hence it is clear that the act of existing (*esse*) is other than essence or quiddity, unless, perhaps, there is a being whose quiddity is its very act of existing. And there can be only one such being, the First Being. . . .Consequently, this excepted, in every other thing the act of existing is other than its quiddity, nature, or form.

Summarizing Statement

All of the foregoing points made to show the necessity of making a "real distinction" between essence and existence in every created being are interrelated. But, for the sake of clarity, we can set forth four different threads of thought which lead us to this conclusion of the "real distinction."

First of all, we can proceed from an analysis of *act* and *potency*. "Act" signifies perfection; and "potency" is the capacity for perfection and its limiting principle. This is true wherever act and potency are found. Now, in the order of being itself, the act of every actual finite being is "to be," or existence. There must be in each such being a corresponding, limiting potency. This is nothing else than their "essence," which is any nature conceivable, *capable* of existing. Thus, essence and existence are related as potency and act in every finite being and must be understood as distinct from each other.

Secondly, we can proceed from the contrast between Infinite Being and finite being. In God alone do we find One whose very nature is to exist. If any actual finite being's nature were the same as its existence, it would be a divine being. This is unacceptable, and hence we say that in every finite being, unlike God, there is a real distinction between its essence and its existence (to be).

Thirdly, we can proceed from the fact that there are many different kinds of finite beings. Each different kind of finite being has a different *essence* from every other kind, e.g., the essence of a dog is not the essence of a tree. But both a tree and a dog (though *different kinds* of being) are alike in the fact that they ARE. Hence, in such kinds of being, there must be a distinction between the fact that they are (their existences) and what they are (their essences).

Finally, we can restrict our starting point to the mere consideration of the meaning of "essence" in a finite being. No such essence that you may think of (e.g., a "phoenix" or a "man") involves "existence," and I can think of them without knowing whether they exist or not. But, if they do exist, existence is a perfection of principle added to their essences.

A Note of Caution

In speaking of the real distinction it is important to realize that we do not consider essence and existence as separate things. They are *principles* of being which are mutually related to each other. The real things we find around us cannot be explained except as composite of these two principles. What is real, therefore, are not the principles taken in isolation or in abstraction from a finite reality, but a total reality as we find it. In our effort to rationally explain such reality, we understand the necessity of two principles. This composition of all finite things of essence and existence is the reason why St. Thomas calls creatures "participated beings." Since they receive existence according to their limited capacities (essences), they radically differ from God, who enjoys the fullness of being. Hence the name of "participation" is sometimes given to the preceding explanation of the difference of finite from infinite being.

Possible Beings

We have been concerned with actually "existing" things, which are composed of potency (essence) and act (existence). Now we must turn our attention to possible things—all those beings which are capable of existing, but do not. They are potencies, capacities for existence. Where are they? Obviously, not in the actual world. They exist only as ideas in our minds. But *our* minds should not be considered the ultimate source of

the possibles, because we cannot conceive or understand all conceivable and intelligible things. Only the
Infinite Mind of God can do that. It is His intellect,
therefore, that is the formal (knowing) source of all
possible things, which He knows in understanding the
Infinity of His own essence. He sees that His Infinite
Essence can be imitated in an infinite number of ways;
and there is no limit to the number of ideas representing
such possible imitations of Himself. Thus, God's Essence
as infinitely imitable is the fundamental source of the
possibles. God's intellect and essence are therefore the
source of the possibles. This doctrine is sometimes
called Exemplarism, and it is very much related to our
previous chapters, as illustrated in the chart below.

ANALOGY OF PROPORTIONALITY: the consideration
of the idea of being as including both Infinite
and finite beings, inasmuch as each represents
a proportion between essence and the "to be"
(infinite in the infinite; finite in the finite).
PARTICIPATION: the view of all actual and finite things
as composed of potency (essence) and act (to
be) in contrast to God, the Pure Act, Whose
Essence is TO BE.
EXEMPLARISM: the view of all possible things as related
to God as Exemplar, because they are the
divine ideas of imitations of the divine essence.

God's Power

God's Will is the source of actual things. God's power is unlimited, and therefore all possibles (conceivable
things) lie within His power. When possibles are considered as the unlimited number of things that can be

done by God, they are called "metaphysically" or absolutely possible. When possibles are referred to man's limited power, we speak of "moral" possibility; and when referred to the powers of nature, we speak of "physical" possibility.

These terms are used frequently in philosophy and hence deserve a brief explanation. Although the terms may vary in their application (they are analogous terms), generally we may say that the "metaphysical" order refers to the suprasensible, unchanging, absolute aspects of both actual and possible things. The "physical" order refers to the sensible and to the natural universe, but sometimes it may include all "actual" things. The "moral" order refers to the realm of man's free activity, and though it depends on man's free execution, nevertheless ultimately refers to the order willed by God. In some contexts, "moral" can take on the meaning, "in the common estimation of men." Finally, the "logical" order generally refers to the order of man's knowledge.

The table below seeks to bring these distinctions out:

METAPHYSICAL: the suprasensible aspects of all actual and possible things
PHYSICAL: the sensible aspects of all actual things
MORAL: the realm of man's free activity, or "according to the common estimation of men"
LOGICAL: the order of man's knowledge

Divisions of Act and Potency

Before concluding the chapter, we should list various

divisions that are in common use among Scholastic philosophers when speaking of act and potency. To distinguish between God (the Uncreated Act) and every created thing (act with some composition of potency), the term *Pure Act* is used for God, and *mixed acts* for creatures. Creatures may also be called *subjective* (real) potencies because, though they are real and hence in some sense act, they are capable of further perfection (potency). Purely possible things are then called *logical* (or "objective") potency.* Subjective potency is usually "passive" (the capacity to receive). "Active" potency is a misnomer, since it means the power to act. In this sense, God's Infinite Power may be called active potency. More frequently, *active power* refers to the limited capacities (operative powers) of created things. The accompanying chart brings this out and will also serve as a summary for the chapter.

---

*The possible, as such, is in the intellectual order, the order of the mind; it is the concept of an essence that can be actualized; in this sense it is midway between "nothing" and actually existing things, as the following table of contrasts shows:

Possibles	*"Nothing"*
−can be actualized	−can never be actualized
−are many	−is not even one
−are positive	−negative
−conceivable	−inconceivable
−distinguishable	−indistinguishable

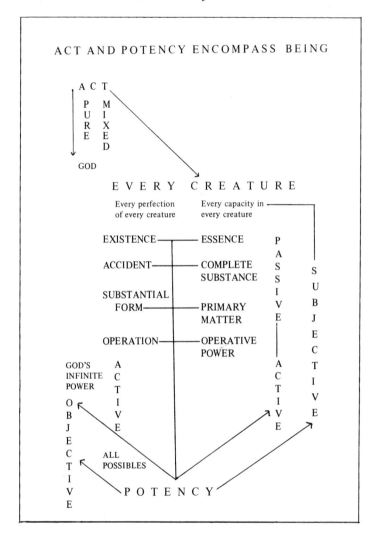

4.

THE INTERRELATED UNIVERSE

Every being is related. We have already seen how every being is *similar* to every other and *similar* to God, Who is the Supreme Exemplar and Cause of all things.[1] Similarity is a *relationship,* implication by one thing of another. No being is understood in isolation and must be seen as similar to every other. Its similarity to others is rooted in its very being by the fact that it exists. Thus, similarity in being is everywhere noticeable, wherever being is present: a necessary relationship, not dependent on our mind or on any accidental contingency.

The Mysteriousness of Being

The Christian existentialist, Gabriel Marcel, refers to being as a mystery. In the sense that a mystery is something which cannot be completely understood, philosophy itself is a proof of Marcel's insight. For, if being were completely understandable, philosophy would have ceased to exist long ago.

In what way can we come to a better understanding of the mysterious character of being or reality? The phrase of St. Thomas, cited in chapter one, is helpful. He refers to being as "absolute actuality." We returned

1. See St. Thomas, *Summa* I, 13, 7.

to this thought also in chapter two. The fact is that beings exist; and this is totally beyond our control, independent of our personal desires or thoughts—a fact to be accepted rather than challenged. Here we are face to face with something that transcends us. However, in regard to every being, as we find it, its absolute character does not completely elude us but presents us with undeniable characteristics which Thomistic philosophy deems all-important. Like being, these characteristics are open to our intellectual gaze, but beyond our control. When we look into any being, which is "absolute" in the sense explained, we find within it (immanent to it) certain traits which account for the similarity of all things among themselves, and these traits must be expressed in terms of "relationships." Though being is absolute and mysterious, there are immanent to it certain characteristics which to some extent we can understand. These consist in certain *relationships.* What are these relationships?

Recall, first of all, we said in the very first chapter that every being denotes the *relationship* of its own essence to existence. Again, every finite being, in which essence and existence are distinct, implies (denotes a *relationship* of dependency to) the Infinite Being as its Cause. Finally, every being bespeaks a *relationship* to mind as something intelligible (truth); and every being denotes a *relationship* to will as something desirable (goodness). This now is to be explained.

The Transcendentals of Being

Thus, every being is similar, not only in the fact that it exists, but also because it always bespeaks certain relationships. It was by a consideration of all these varying aspects of being that St. Thomas derived the so-called "transcendentals of being," which we must take up during the course of this book. By "transcendentals" St. Thomas meant precisely the various aspects under which "being" can be considered. They are not realities distinct from being, but being itself considered from all possible angles. We derive the transcendentals of being in the following way.

Considered in itself, each being has an essence (quiddity or whatness) making it what it is. This is the ordinary name for being, viz., *thing.* Secondly, every being is *itself,* undivided in itself, or *one* thing and only one. In this sense, we call every being *one.* Then, considered relatively, as we have seen, every being can be considered in relation to mind, i.e., as something intelligible, actually known to God and potentially knowable by any intellect (True). Likewise, in relation to will, every thing can be considered as something desirable, actually willed by God and capable of being desired by other wills or appetites (Good). Furthermore, every being can be considered as distinct from every other thing, i.e., as *another* thing, or other. The word we use to designate this aspect of being is "something else" (in Latin, *aliquid*). Hence there are five transcendentals of being: thing, one, true, good, something.

The terms, thing and something, seem so synonymous with being itself that they are taken for granted. But the other terms, *unity, truth* and *goodness* are called the transcendental *properties* of being because they seem to bring out explicitly the characteristics which, as it were, lie hidden in being. Thus, unity explicitly expresses the

undividedness of being, truth the *intelligibility* of being
(relationship to intellect) and goodness the *desirability*
of being (relationship to will).

As we proceed, chapter by chapter, we will consider
each of the transcendentals and the transcendental properties, as well as the Categories of Aristotle, which
correspond to them.

Importance of Relationship

From the foregoing, it is very clear that "relationship"
is a very important and all-pervading aspect of reality.
Actually "relationship" is so much a part of our experience of reality and of knowledge that it is as well-known
to us as being itself. Therefore, it is impossible strictly
to define it. We can only describe it. Relationship
means "implication of another." Something is "relative"
if it implies another, as for example, a "father" implies
a "son." Examples might be given without limit, for
the amplitude of relation is practically endless. We
have been speaking, in fact, almost constantly of many
different kinds of relationships from the very first
pages of this book: the relationship between essence and
existence, between matter and form and between substance and accident, which we said were *related* as
potency to act. The very act of knowledge, by which
we know anything, is constituted by a *relation* of our
mind to reality. And throughout this chapter we have
been saying that not only does "relationship" come into
our analysis of being itself (which is the *relationship*
of essence to existence), but it comes into play when we
derive the transcendentals of being, which must be considered as *related* to mind (true), *related* to will (good)

and distinct (*related* by contrast, or other) from anything else.

Further Development

From the foregoing considerations we can draw up a
series of tables about being, and about the similarity
between Infinite and finite being, between substantial
and accidental being. In the first table, we set down the
transcendentals and the transcendental properties together with certain basic perfections in every being,
which the transcendentals imply.

1	2	3	4	5	Row
Infinite Power	Being	Goodness	Existence	Act	A
Infinite Intelligence	Thing	Truth	Essence	Potency	B
Infinite Spirit	One and No Other	Unity	Subsistence	Substance	C

TABLE ONE: THE TRANSCENDENTALS
(Explanations of each column and row follow)

Column 1: Names and aspects of the Supreme Being, GOD.

Column 2: Names for every reality, the "transcendentals," synonyms of "being."

Column 3: "Transcendental properties" of being, aspects of being
which express explicitly what is implicit in being.

Column 4: Ontological factors or principles which are necessary
in the makeup of every finite being. Existence and
essence have already been considered. Subsistence
will be treated in the next chapter.

Column 5: Aspects and proper designations for every finite being of the substantial order.

Row A: The aspects or principles of being in Row A should be understood in terms of the Infinity of the Divine Will and of the consequent action of the Divine Will.

Row B: The aspects or principles of being in Row B should be understood in terms of the Infinity of Divine Intelligence and Its creativity. However, this creativity is counterbalanced by the potentiality, finitude and perfectibility of the creature.

Row C: The aspects or principles of being in Row C should be understood in terms of the Infinity of God's Being as Spirit, and His uniqueness, which is imitated by each creature as far as possible.

We can further develop our understanding of being and its various aspects, as just sketched, if we pause briefly and study the first principles of knowledge (which are sometimes called the *transcendental principles*), which are immediately understood to govern all being. The first of these principles is the *principle of contradiction.* It can be expressed in three formulas. Its simplest formulation is called the "principle of identity" and is stated very simply: *Whatever is, is.* The second expression of the principle is called the "principle of the excluded middle" and is stated as follows: *Either a thing is or is not* (there is no midway between being and nothing). But the most complete and the most ordinary way to enunciate the principle of contradiction is in the following way: *A thing cannot be and not be at the same time and under the same aspect.*

There are three other principles related to the principle of contradiction. These are: (1) *Action follows upon being (agere sequitur esse)*, which means that every being has its proper activity, proportionate to its nature, by which it can be known. (2) *There must be a sufficient reason for every being* (the principle of sufficient reason). (3) *Wherever two things agree with a third, they must agree among themselves; and whenever, of two things, one is in agreement with a third and the other is not, they do not agree among themselves* (principle of agreement and disagreement).

In understanding these principles and in understanding being itself, there are certain basic ideas which the human intellect naturally forms. Thus, in understanding *action*, the intellect understands the meaning of an agent and of the end (or purpose) of an action. With spontaneous conviction, the intellect can say: *there is purpose in every action*, or *every agent acts for an end* (the principle of finality). Similarly, the intellect naturally forms the ideas of *effect* and *cause* in considering the recipient of an action, reversing its point of view. *If something is done or made, it must be done by an agent or cause* (principle of causality). Finally, the mind can naturally understand the difference between substance and accident (see page 29) and say: *either a thing is a substance or an accident* (principle of substantiality).

We can now enlarge the chart on page 55 to include the foregoing. We will not repeat the explanations of columns one to five. While we explicitly explain each new column, proceeding in each case vertically, we should not lose sight of the relationships that exist between the various items taken horizontally in each line of the table.

1	2-5	6	7	8	9
Infinite Power	Being Goodness Existence Act	Principle of Identity	*Agere Sequitur Esse*	Agent-End	Principle of Finality
Infinite Intelligence	Thing Truth Essence Potency	Principle of Contradiction	Principle of Sufficient Reason	Effect-Cause	Principle of Causality
Infinite Spirit	Other Unity Subsistence Substance	Principle of the Excluded Middle	Principle of Agreement and Disagreement	Substance Accident	Principle of Substantiality

TABLE TWO: THE TRANSCENDENTAL PRINCIPLES

(See Table One, pages 55-56, for explanations.)

Column 6: The first principles of knowledge, understood to govern all reality.

Column 7: Other principles closely related to the very knowledge of being.

Column 8: Fundamental ideas immediately evident from being.

Column 9: Primordial certitudes linked to the very knowledge of reality.

N.B. All these principles may be referred to as the *Transcendental Principles,* or *First Principles of Human Knowledge,* which necessarily flow from the knowledge of being itself.

The Categories of Aristotle

In his effort to understand reality, Aristotle listed, together with substance, nine accidents: quantity, quality, relation, action, passion, space, time, posture and habit. These are the most general divisions of being in the accidental order. Instead of considering these accidents separately and by themselves, we have chosen to treat the most important of them in conjunction with each of the transcendentals, which we will take up in the following chapters. For, upon examination, the intellect can see a certain similarity running through the categories by which they resemble the transcendentals and are related to the transcendental principles. Table Three will bring this out, but it should be studied in conjunction with Tables One and Two. Although a complete understanding of Table Three would require our anticipating of treatment of the categories to be given in subsequent chapters, the following observations should be made at this time.

The accidental manifestation of a being's perfection (act) is especially in its *action*. The sensible manifestation of a thing's structure or makeup is especially in its *qualities*, which express what it is. Finally, the singularity of each material thing is manifested by the unity of its parts (*quantity*) in the sensible order. From these three categories of action, quality and quantity arise many relationships of the real and mental orders, by which we understand reality. Accordingly, the concepts of *time, passion,* and *space* also originate.

1 Infinite Power	2 - 3 - 5 - 9 Being-Good-Act-Finality	10 Action	R E L A T I O N S	11 Time
Infinite Intelligence	Thing-True-Potency-Causality	Qualities		Passion
Infinite Spirit	One-Other-Substance-Substantiality	Quantity		Space

TABLE THREE: THE CATEGORIES OF ARISTOTLE
AS RELATED TO THE TRANSCENDENTALS

Column 10: Corresponding categories of being in the accidental order. (1) Every created being within our experience is an act whose end is in some activity, which is measured in time and productive of many cause-effect relationships. (2) Every (created) thing is an intelligible potency, subject to causality and manifesting itself through its qualities and corresponding relationships. (3) Every "one" is other than every other substance; and, if material, has a union of parts which are manifested in space. Besides, each being is related to other beings in manifold relationships because of quantity.

Column 11: As is studied in Cosmology, space and time are "beings of reason," which result from our observation and universalization of extension (quantity) and of change (action) and from the mutual relationships arising from changing, extended bodies. *Passion* is the reception of action with which it is identified, but seen from a different point of view. *"Actio est in passo."*

5.

UNITY

In this chapter we will study an aspect of being which we generally take for granted—the fact that each thing is *one* thing. As we saw from the very beginning, being itself primarily denotes an existing thing: it refers to the perfection of existence. "Thing" denotes the essential make-up of a reality, its nature, which can be represented in a concept of what the thing is. *"One"* introduces us into the mystery of *singular* being. Every being, besides having a nature and an existence, is unique.

Ontological Uniqueness of Each Thing

We are here considering a very intricate metaphysical question, one that has caused a great deal of philosophical speculation. In our times, though refusing to speculate on the matter, the Existentialists devote their whole attention to "the subject," the existing and singular being, especially the individual human being. In traditional language, they are interested in "the supposit," especially intellectual ones, viz., persons. In the philosophy of St. Thomas this aspect of a being is of the utmost importance and is usually treated under the heading of *supposit* or *person.*

By "supposit" St. Thomas means *someone distinct* in some nature. He means a really existing, singular and complete substance, such as my dog, Fido, or any other substantial thing really existing. You can *name* and *number* it, because it is some one thing that is unique and set off from every other thing.

If the being in question is of an intellectual nature, we have a person, i.e., someone distinct in an intellectual nature. Now the question that arises at this point of philosophical inquiry is: how do we account for the unicity of each supposit or each person? Existence cannot account for this aspect of a being, because existence is the perfection of the "to be," which makes all things alike, as we have seen. Existence answers the question: is it? On the other hand, *essence* does not give the answer to our present question either. Essence tells us *what a thing is* and is thought of as common to many of the same group, as for example "man" is an idea we can apply to all men. Essence answers the question: what is it? But, after we answer the questions, "Is it?" and "What is it?" about any substantial being, there remains a deeper question: "Who is it?" or "Which one is it?" There is a characteristic in each thing that makes it unique and only one—the most mysterious aspect of a thing. This characteristic, unique in each individual thing, is called by St. Thomas "subsistence." Webster's dictionary takes note of this concept and, in one of its entries, describes it as follows: something by which an *individual* (as individual) is what it is; in other words, that which constitutes an individual as individual.

Subsistence

So, we have in each being of the real and substantial order, three principles of being without which an individual being would be impossible: essence, subsistence and existence. We cannot think of a real existing substance without these principles, but they must be correctly conceived. "Existence" should be thought of in terms of *action*—the "to be"—the fact that a thing IS. "Essence" must be thought of in terms of an idea intelligible to our minds, i.e., in terms of the basic structure of a definite kind of thing. "Subsistence" is the most mysterious of all because it represents what is most unique, singular and proper to each thing, e.g., *me* as *me*. There must be something in me which makes me myself and no other; and this cannot be the same as my humanity (essence) or my being (existence). Otherwise, every man and every being would be me! As a little boy once put it, in a flash of intuition not uncommon in children, "I keep trying to think that I am somebody else, but I'm always myself." In other words, it is possible to think of many perfections that I have in common with others, which make me like them, but one thing is proper to me alone—my own self as myself. This is my individual personality or distinctiveness, or in philosophical language, my *subsistence.* Perhaps we can represent subsistence by a *number,* in the sense that each distinct being, if enumerated, would be a different number.

As we think of "to be" (existence) in terms of action, we should also ultimately explain it in terms of God's Will or Action, by which He calls into being each thing and makes it continue in existence. Similarly, as *essence* can be embodied in a concept of our own mind, ultimately it is traced back to God's intellect understanding His own essence as imitable. Finally, as subsistence is representable by a number, so its ultimate explanation carries us back to God as the Mysterious *Some One,* Who is at the origin of all things. We have to go back to the Original One who necessarily IS. No *one* can be understood except in relation to *That One.* Everyone must be understood, therefore, as a *relative* of Him, without Whom in the first place there would have been no Being at all.

Philosophically, then, each supposit (each person) must be defined in terms of a unique relationship to the One Principle.   Theologically, this One Principle is known to be God the Father, Who necessarily implies God the Son and the Spirit of Love proceeding from both.   These two distinct Ones have a necessary relationship to God the Father. All other (freely created) beings have a gratuitous relationship to Him and consequently to the Other Two Persons. But even philosophically, we can see in each created being a triple relationship to God. By subsistence each thing is a distinct and finite imitation of (relationship to) God as the Only Infinite One in Being. By essence, each thing has a relationship to God's Infinite Intelligence. By existence, each thing denotes a relationship to God's Infinite Good Will by which it was called into existence and in fact continues to be. It is not surprising that, in the three principles of essence, subsistence and existence, following the Doctors of the Church, we might detect a "vestige" of the Holy Trinity.[1]   It would be

---

1. See St. Augustine, *De Trinitate* 6, 10; *De Natura Boni,* 3. St. Thomas, *Summa* I, 45, 7. St. Bonaventure, *Itinerarium Mentis in Deum,* VI, 3. Although expressed in different ways, the main thought of the Doctors is this: each creature is a new, distinct mystery in being: it is someone who

beyond the scope of this philosophical work to elaborate upon this point. Suffice it to say that, philosophically speaking, there are three synonyms for every entity: *being, thing* and one (thing), and no other, which are expressed by Saint Thomas Aquinas as *ens, res et aliquid.*[2] Although these are just words for the same thing, three distinct principles of being or three positive perfections are implied as present in each thing: essence, singularity (subsistence) and existence.

Summarizing Remarks on Subsistence

At the risk of belaboring the point, we are going to include here some summarizing statements telling why we consider subsistence as different from both existence and essence in all finite beings.

(1) Existence cannot account for two contrary effects, viz., *TO BE* and *TO BE DIFFERENT* from every other as singular, subsistent and distinct. But existence accounts for *TO BE.* Hence another principle (viz., subsistence) is needed to account for singularity and distinctiveness. On the other hand, this principle (subsistence) cannot be identical to *nature,* because nature is common to many. St. Thomas writes:

> ...clearly no individual can share with others its very singularity. Socrates can share what makes him

---

is not God but related to Him, who (though mysterious) can to some extent be understood, and who exists.

2. We are taking "aliquid" here in a wide sense as including a thing's basic unity as described in the text above. St. Thomas does not use the word, *unum* (one), in this context and treats it in the purely negative meaning of "undividedness" mentioned on page 53 and to be explained in the next chapter. It is St. Bonaventure who stresses the positive aspect of *one*; but we have interpreted this in the light of the principles of St. Thomas.

man with many others, but what makes him this man can belong to one alone. So if Socrates were this man just by being a man, there could no more be many men than there could be many Socrates. *Summa,* I, 11, 3.

(2) Being, abstractly considered, signifies essence and existence. Both these notions are *common:* Existence is *common* to all Actual Beings, including God; essence, as distinguished from existence, is *common* to all creatures. However, bringing being down to the concrete order, it must include that which distinguishes one being from another, i.e., the *unique relationship* which each essence has to its existence. In the case of persons, there is *someone referred* to exist in an intellectual nature, and this *reference* or this *someone referred* is over and above (distinguishable, though not separable, from) essence and existence. It is this very *singular* element in a person that we designate by the abstract terminology, *substantial mode* or *subsistence.*

(3) As the distinction between essence and existence establishes the fundamental difference between creatures and their Creator, so the distinction between subsistence and existence establishes the fundamental difference of creatures among themselves as "distinct *ones.*"

(4) Each thing resembles God, as the doctrine of exemplarism brings out. But the resemblance of each thing to God must be borne out on three levels:

(a) Each thing's essence is a finite imitation of God's infinite essence, modelled on one of His ideas.

(b) Each thing resembles God by be-ing, i.e., by the act of existence.

(c) Each thing resembles God by being something *distinct.*

Thus a person is a *relative* of God (like everything else) not merely as BEING, but as SOMEONE DISTINCT WITH AN INTELLECTUAL NATURE.

(5) Subsistence is the reference point to Pure Being and, at the same time, the principle by which we are withdrawn from Pure Being.

It is the principle by which all created beings ultimately are distinguishable from each other. The real distinction between essence and existence sets off all creatures from the Creator. Each creature's own subsistence sets it off from every other creature.

(a) Existence may be considered as the principle accounting for the *being* and *goodness* of a thing (*ens et bonum*).

(b) Essence accounts for the *kind of thing* and its *truth* or intelligibility (*res et verum*).

(c) Subsistence accounts for the fact that a thing is *one* (singular) and an *other* from everything else (*unum et aliquid*).

(d) While distinct in creatures, these three principles are identical in God alone, Who is the *One* whose *nature* is *to be.*

(6) Supposit embodies:

(a) Relationship to God, as similar in existence; as imitation in essence; *as distinct in subsistence.*

(b) The *unique* relationship of essence to existence.

(c) Relationship of matter to form (in corporeal things).

Supposit (as naturally ONE and a basic unit, complete in itself) EXCLUDES all accidental and artificial units, all mere conglomerations.

Quotations Showing the Mystery of Person, Especially Its Relational Connotation

1. The notion of personality thus involves that of wholeness and independence. To say that a man is a person is to say that in the depth of his being he is more a whole than a part and more independent than servile. It is this mystery of our nature which religious thought designates when it says that the person is the image of God. A person possesses absolute dignity because he is in direct relationship with the realm of being, truth, goodness, and beauty, and with God, and it is only with these that he can arrive at his complete fulfillment. Jacques Maritain, *Education At the Crossroads* (Yale University Press, New Haven, 1943), p. 8.

2. The Category of Relation is neither per se substance nor accident but as it may be required. Person is essentially a being *ad alium.* Paul Henry, S. J., *St. Augustine on Personality,* (Macmillan, N. Y., 1960), p. 19.

3. The name person is a term taken from the ancient theater. In ancient comedies and tragedies actors wore a mask which was called a "persona," since their voices "sounded through" (*personare*) the mask. In giving directions to the actors the playwrights felt that the natural features of the actors and actresses should not appear, for this would take away the dignity befitting the part they played. The name person was later transferred to men. We do not know why. Perhaps it lay in the fact that the actors on the stage usually represented

noble men. Perhaps this term was applied to men because every human being is in his deepest being inscrutable, like one wearing a mask. Perhaps there is a mask over one's personality so that no one can see behind it even when he looks into the mirror of his own conscience. Whatever the correct historical explanation of the transfer of the name to men, it is true that each one of us is a mystery behind a mask that reveals very little of our inner self. H. Reith, *The Metaphysics of St. Thomas Aquinas,* (Bruce, Milwaukee, 1958), p. 107.

4. ...the discrepancy in man between the meaning of his existence and his actual existence grows clear to us. It begins to dawn on us that no question can find an answer in man alone, that the strangeness of human existence becomes intolerable unless it is grounded in God. Already St. Augustine is preparing the ground for the decisive realization that a man that surrenders himself to God is not surrendering himself to someone else, because for his creature God is never "someone else," but God, his Creator; because God is He Who is, the more He prevails in a creature the more He brings him into his own true existence. It is only through the personal God that man becomes essentially PERSON. R. Guardini, *Conversion of Augustine,* (Newman, Westminster, Md., 1960), p. 94.

5. From this, that the humanity and this man differ in such fashion that the former, in reality, is capable neither of the act of existing, nor of real relationship, except by reason of *this* man as the *per se primo* subject of both, we must admit that there is some real difference between this humanity and this man, so that man includes something real that this humanity does not in-

clude. *Summa,* III, 4, 2, Commentary by Cajetan.

Numerical Unity

The consideration of being as singular led us to postulate "subsistence" as a positive perfection in each substantial thing. Now we must turn our attention to an equally impressive kind of unity found in material things—a unity based on quantity or plurality of parts. We see that each material thing is one, even though it has a plurality of parts.

Matter of its very nature implies quantity, which basically consists of *parts,* whether we consider these parts as entering into the very constitution of matter itself, or as a necessary adjunct or as only virtually inherent in matter.[3] In any case, quantity is a necessary characteristic of matter. The importance of quantity, in fact, is shown by its position as the first predicament or category listed among the accidents by Aristotle. It is quantity which, not only gives parts to a material substance, but unity of parts among themselves. In our sensible experience, we can verify this unity of parts, which we find localized, divisible, measurable and mutually impenetrable. Even if these latter characteristics were removed, however, a material thing would still require a basic unity of parts bestowed by quantity.[4] Presupposing the previous substantial unity, this is an additional and indispensable unity.

---

3. The first position is that of the Franciscan School, the second is that of Sylvester of Ferrara and the third of Cajetan.

4. Quantity, in this basic sense, is sometimes called, *intrinsic* quantity or extension. Localized quantity (as we usually find it) is called *extrinsic* extension.

Consider, for example, how important this kind of unity is for a man. For no *one* man can exist without parts, for these naturally spring from the fact that he is a material kind of being. This characteristic, then, is necessary for a man and pertains to his nature as corporeal. Furthermore, it is this principle which makes possible the multiplication of many individuals within the same species. Hence, we may say that the material principle in man, marked by quantity, both manifests the man in space and allows for the multiplication of individuals within the species. St. Thomas calls quantity in this sense *the principle of individuation,* but this is to be taken as the outward *manifestation* of individuation. Every being must be first unique and individual in itself, and then, if material, possess a unity of parts through quantity. Then this twofold unity can be manifested externally. If a being is material and has parts, these parts manifest a uniqueness already constituted, while displaying a new unity of parts in the accidental or sensible order. It is this kind of unity that daily confronts us in material things, which originates from the plurality of parts in quantity, and which gives rise to the Science of Mathematics. This is sometimes called numerical and predicamental unity; and though its source is indeed in quantity, nevertheless it points to a much more mysterious unity (despite plurality of principles) in every created being as it falteringly reveals the Mystery of Infinite Being.

Proper and Improper Unity

We have been speaking of *unity,* both in the metaphysical and physical orders. In either order, this kind of unity (of *one* thing, whether spiritual or material) is called *proper* unity. The unity of several things is improper or *accidental* unity, such as a union of a group of free persons (moral unity), the unity of many things brought together under one concept (logical unity), the unity resulting from man's artifice (e.g., a house) which is called artificial unity, and the unity resulting from pure coincidence or some contingency (e.g., a pile of stones) which is a purely accidental unity.

The following chart sums up these distinctions:

Kinds of Unity

Proper: the unity of one thing (*metaphysical* or *physical*).

Improper: the unity of several things—*moral,* or *logical,* or *artificial,* or purely *accidental.*

See Appendix One for a further elaboration.

6.

DIFFERENCE

There are various aspects of unity. When we say "unity," we can refer to its absolute and positive meaning, as explained in the preceding chapter. Or, we may refer to its absolute and *negative* character, which is the sense usually employed by St. Thomas. Here "one" merely means "undivided," that is to say, *not* 2, *not* 3, *not* 4, etc. There is very little to say about this aspect of being except that it is a property of every being, as we pointed out on page 53.[1]

But "one" can also be taken in the sense of "one and no other." In this sense, it is synonymous with *something else,* or *aliquid* in the meaning presently to be explained: *aliquid* as denoting the *otherness* or difference of one thing from another. It is in this sense that St. Thomas usually understands "aliquid." [2]

---

1. Lest we be misunderstood by the "experts" in Metaphysics, we should point out that we are speaking here *in the order of being.* We are not *enumerating* beings of the same kind in the material order; but we are concerned with distinct beings in the metaphysical order, wherein every being is undivided in itself and therefore able to be set off from every other being. See St. Thomas, *Summa,* I, 11, 1.

2. In the preceding chapter we considered the hidden and subtle *unity* that "something" presupposes. Here we are considering the explicit meaning of "something." Again, we will employ the principles of St. Thomas, though he teaches the content of this chapter in a different context.

When we say that each thing is "something else," we are saying that such thing is *not* anything else (negative aspect).   And at the same time, we are saying that the thing is *other than* anything else (relative aspect).   The relationship employed here is not one of similarity, but of dissimilarity or contrast.   No being is any other.

The Relationship Involved Here

There is no end to the possible considerations which might arise from being as related.   We have seen, in fact, that the very meaning of being itself is an essence *related to existence.*   We also saw that "true" means being as *related* to mind.   Likewise, goodness means being as *related* to will or appetite.   Now, we are considering being as "other," a relation of dissimilarity.   In any case, we may note again that "relation" is somehow included in the understanding of the transcendentals.

God, The Infinite Being, as Other

God, Who is infinitely Other from every possible and every actual creature or finite being is the "Other" par excellence.   St. Thomas says: "We only know God truly when we realize that He is above all that man can think about God" (*Contra Gentiles,* 1, 5).   His Being and His Goodness surpass our understanding.   Hence He is the Supremely Other, the Absolutely Selfless One, Who giving everything to everyone, is the Necessary One, to Whom all are, and must be, related.   Though He is the supreme Mystery, His ways are not completely mysterious, for they stand revealed in the generous works of His creation.   Hence we can understand something of Him by considering His work, the material things as well as the spiritual aspects of our own human nature, for God is a Spirit. Furthermore, we must consider God as He reveals Himself in the Universe at large, in the "totality of being," at which He is the Center. As the Supreme Good, He relates all things to Himself and among themselves, individually and collectively. The relationships which He establishes in the physical world can be known to man; and man can build upon them for the world's development. The relationships which He wishes man to establish among themselves can also be known to man's conscience and is the subject matter of Ethics. These relationships can be known to man in addition to God's personal revelation of Himself through the Man, Jesus Christ, whose way of life and thought has changed and is changing the world, for no thinker in history has so transformed the world.

The Man for Others

The whole process of transformation of the world, in fact, calls for an immanent Principle, other than the world as such, Who is capable of corelating all things, on the metaphysical, physical, intellectual and moral levels of reality. Such a One, according to Christian thought, is Christ Himself, the God-made-Man, Who remains Other to all creation in His Person, yet on every level of reality is at the center of the manifold order in the universe. He is not only the Other par excellence, but the Man for Others, Who relates all things to God.

It is not our task to consider the relationships of the moral order which find their origin in the historical Christ. Prior to such relationships, and on a level open to the intellect of every man, are the relationships in the world at large, which called for a Creative Intelligence to explain the transcendental order in the world—that order that includes the overlapping realms of the ontological, physical and human orders.

A first and necessary step in this direction is the admission of *order* itself as a genuine fact open to human intelligence, an order which is nothing less than a vast network of relationships. Consider the transcendental relationships of truth and goodness in all things. Identified with being itself, these are everywhere present and necessarily make all things similar. Or consider the basic relationships between the principles of being as such, viz., those between act and potency, between essence and existence, between substance and accident and between matter and form. These are also called transcendental relationships because they are so basic to being. Finally, consider the so-called accidental or predicamental relations, the third category listed by Aristotle.

The Nature of Accidental Relationship

It is an essential task of Metaphysics to study the fact of accidental relationships. First of all, it is necessary to define the meaning of such relationships. These are the *connections* existing among some things, such as the *link* between a father and his son, the "equality" between two things with the same measurement of quantity, the "similarity" between several accidental characteristics in several different persons, etc. In all these examples we are face to face with realities completely beyond the grasp of the senses and understandable to the intellect alone. What are these strange realities? We ought not try to imagine such beings, for as we have remarked, neither external sense nor imagination can know relation.

Indeed, Father Renard explains, this "imagining" has been the source of many of the vicissitudes which the concept of predicamental relation has undergone. Some of the philosophers of the past four centuries could only laugh at those innumerable little beings of the earlier scholastics (*entitatulae*, they called them), which seemed to be flying around at a terrific speed, and which were so elastic as to stretch indefinitely. Such, for example, they said would be the elasticity of the relation between father and son, as soon as the father or the son would move away from the other. Henri Renard, *The Philosophy of Being* (Bruce, Milwaukee, 1946), p. 251.

Of course, it is a mistake to think of relationships as if they were complete realities. Like essence and existence in the substantial order, so predicamental relation (in the accidental order) is only a *principle* of being, not a reality in itself. St. Thomas calls it *debilissimum ens* (the weakest of all beings), because the slightest change can cause the destruction of such relations. Think of the exact timing and the precise relationships or connections which must be established and maintained for a successful flight to the moon. Again, in the words of Fr. Renard:

Today it is interesting to note that in the world of physics, we find that electric waves travel at unimaginable speed, that their number is beyond comprehension. And while in no way admitting a comparison in the strict sense between such physical entities and predicamental relation which is only a principle of being, it is amusing to realize that one of the greatest difficulties proposed against the reality of relation by physico-philosophers of a past age has absolutely no meaning in a world of atoms and electrons. (*Ibid.*)

The Factors in a Relation

There are three factors which come into a relation called (1) the *subject,* which is related (e.g., a father), (2) the *term* to which the subject is related (e.g., a son) and (3) the foundation for the relation (e.g., the act of generation). In the above example, we have a cause-effect relationship, based on action. There are hundreds of unnamed relationships of this kind. Mathematics could supply us with thousands of examples of relationships based on quantity. Finally, quality can be the cause of similarity and other relationships among things. The natural sciences explore these relationships.

St. Thomas insists on the objectivity of relationships of these kinds among things. Indeed, such relationships constitute the real order in the world. "Order" is nothing else than a complexus of relationships which are rooted in the real world, which the human mind can detect, and without which the world would be unintelligible. In a word, without real relationships in the world, there would be chaos. Similarly, without a Supreme Ordainer and Communicator of all these re-

lationships, it is impossible to explain either the relationships in the world at large or their discovery by
men.

Kinds of Relations

Before concluding the chapter, we should speak of the
various kinds of relations of both the substantial and
accidental orders. "Relation" per se does not denote
either a substance or an accident, but may refer to
either.

A relative or relation is someone or something which
implies another. Every created being is, in this sense, a
relative of God and of all things. Thus, relationship has
a quasi-transcendental amplitude. The term, correctly
interpreted, may even refer to God and is, in fact, used
in Theology.

A relation is called real, if it exists independently of
the mind, logical if it is a result of human convention
(e.g., an olive branch considered as related to peace). A
relation is called transcendental, if it is necessary (the
relationships involved in transcendental truth and goodness as well as the relationships between the principles
of being) and accidental, if it is contingent upon some
accident (quantity, quality, action-passion).

The mysteriousness of God is reflected from the
beginning to the end of created reality. If every substantial being expresses a relationship to God, the connections existing between created substances and arising
from their own characteristics and activities are *relationships*—vague hints of the Trinity in God, as briefly
explained on the following, concluding pages of this
chapter.

The Trinity and Relation

In the Blessed Trinity, according to Catholic Faith, the Three Persons are Subsisting Relations. The distinction of the Persons rests on the distinctiveness of their relationships to each other. Catholic philosophers draw an analogy from this truth. There are subsisting relations in the Trinity, which is a perfect Unity. So also, amid the various realities of the world, the universe forms a kind of unity comparable to the One God. In this universe, however, there are *accidental relations* by which the distinctiveness of things is discernible. In God perfect order requires that God understand and love Himself (with the consequent Subsisting Relations). In the universe there is reflected an order by which things are understood in relation to each other and by which they act and react upon each other, with the resulting accidental relationships.

The unity of the world therefore consists in a complexus of relationships by which things are related to one another and to God. The universe constitutes a Whole of which God is the Center. Although this Whole does not form one substance but is a multitude, it is united into one by reason of the Divine Presence and by the real relationships that connect all things together, both transcendental and accidental.

BEING

unity - relationships

Quotations from St. Thomas on God, the Source of the transcendentals and of all relationships.

UNITY—Just as God Himself is One, so He also produces unity; not only because each thing is one in itself, but also because all things in a certain sense are one perfect unity. *De Potentia,* 3, 16 and I.

TRUTH—Creatures do not reflect their exemplar in a perfect manner. Hence, they can reflect it in many ways, and there are many images. *De Potentia,* 3, 16 and 12.

DEUS
OPTIMUS
MAXIMUS

GOODNESS—All creatures participate in the divine goodness, with the result that they pour forth to others the goodness which they themselves possess. For it belongs to the nature of goodness to communicate itself to others. S.T., 106, 4.

RELATION—The order of the parts of the universe to each other exists in virtue of the order of the whole universe to God. *De Potentia,* 7, 9.

The Relationship of All Things to God

From the preceding, it is clear that creatures are related to God and to each other in manifold ways by both transcendental and accidental relationships. This will become clearer by the following considerations:

A transcendental relation is a necessary one, of the very nature of the thing in question. Examples:

(a) Between the principles of being: act and potency, etc.

(b) Between the creature and God: since every creature by the very fact that it is, is *similar* to God. Every creature partly manifests God—shows in some way what God is like.

(c) Between creatures among themselves. Every creature as being is *similar* to every other creature as well as to God. (Analogy of Proportionality.)

A predicamental relation is an accidental one (one that is not necessary). Since this relation is not of the very nature of the thing, it *springs from* either the nature of the thing or from some accident. Examples:

(a) Effect-cause relationship: the relation of a son to his father; of a creature to Creator, as *dependent*. (Analogy of Attribution.)

(b) Relationships of equality or the like, based on quantity.

The relationships of creatures to the Creator must not be conceived as *static,* but as dynamic and capable of increase. For this reason, Teilhard de Chardin speaks of a buildup of relationships, by which the universe is ever more closely united with God. He distinguishes various stages in this evolutionary process. In its final stages he refers to it as *trinitization.*

7.

THE TRUE

The order in the world, as we have seen in the preceding chapter, is constituted by the myriad relationships existing among things which make the whole universe one thing. This global unity postulates a Supreme Ordainer, Who relates all things to each other and to their Final End.

Besides global unity, there is the singular oneness in each thing, which every being possesses and which we have accounted for by the positive perfection of subsistence. In addition to this positive oneness in each thing, there is another aspect to unity, which St. Thomas draws from the negative consideration of being as "undivided." Together with unity, taken in this negative sense, the Angelic Doctor lists two other "properties" of being—two new aspects of being, which need further elaboration. They are *truth* and *goodness*—or the *true* and the *good*. The *good* we will consider in the next chapter, and in this chapter the *true*.

"What is true?" A ready answer can be given: whatever is, is true. When someone says that he wants "to know the truth," he means that he wants to know things, or to know conditions, "as they really are." Now everything which is, really is whatever it is, and hence is true. In the famous phrase of St. Augustine, even a fraud is true, because it is truly *that.* The difficulty for us is that we do not know all things as they are, since our minds are finite; and things do not depend on us for their being. But the case is different for God, Who created all things and knows them as corresponding to His creative plan. There is a necessary correspondence of things with the Creative Intellect of God, and this is their truth. Truth, then, is the necessary relationship of all things to the mind of God. Truth, in this sense, is called *ontological, objective, fundamental* and *transcendental.* In this sense, everything is true. Everything lies open to the vision of God.

But all things, which are based on God's creative ideas and therefore correspond to them, exhibit an intelligibility, design, pattern or structure that lie open to any intellect. Things are *knowable* to us. Secondarily, then, and potentially, all things are true for man.

Logical Truth

When, however, man comes to know the truth of things, a new condition arises in man's mind. His mind corresponds to the truth of things. This truth, reflected in the mind of man and consisting in the correspondence of man's ideas with things, is called *logical truth.* This kind of truth is limited. It is a quality existing in man's mind. Though existing *in* man's mind and therefore accidental, it is very important.

In fact, it is the very purpose of philosophy and of science to communicate truth, i.e., knowledge. However, as experience tells us, in the great effort of mankind to come into the possession of ever greater truth, the individual and society may fall into *error,* i.e., their ideas and judgments may not correspond to the truth of things. This lack of correspondence, this lack of real knowledge, is called *falsity.*

To acquire truth, man must seek to know things as they really are. This often requires continuous inquiry and sustained effort.

Qualities

In understanding reality, an important point to remember is that we can learn about things especially by observing their *qualities,* which greatly manifest what things are. As all things are in themselves true, and are manifested in us through the *quality* of knowledge, it is through the category of "quality" that we can learn a great deal of truth about things themselves. Therefore, Aristotle enumerates quality as the second accidental category, placing it immediately after quantity.

Quality has a vast range of meaning. Generally, it refers to any determination or perfection of a substance over and above its basic constituent elements. This could almost refer to any accident, but in the strict meaning of *quality,* the eight other modifications of substance, as listed by Aristotle, are understood to be excluded. Aristotle himself gives four examples of quality, which clarify his meaning. These are: habit and disposition; capacity and incapacity; affections and affective qualities; and form and figure.

A *disposition* is any inclination by which a subject is served well or ill in its nature, viz., good health or its opposite. A habit is a relatively stable disposition rendering a subject's *operations* easier, more prompt and more pleasant, i.e., making them as it were a second nature. Examples of habit: intellectual virtues (science, prudence, art), moral virtues and manual skills.   All habits presuppose the *power* (faculty, capacity) to act in a given area, which brings us to our second division.

A capacity or *operative power* renders a subject capable of activity of a specific kind: thus, intellect, imagination, will and the like are capacities through which the subject receives (exercises) the activities of these faculties.   If the capacity is undermined or weakened, it is called "incapacity."

Affections and *affective qualities* are qualities which produce, or are produced by, sensible alteration. Some authors therefore call them *sensible qualities;* and these include the sensible qualities of bodies and the bodily temperaments and passions (feelings and emotions).

Finally, with respect to continuous quantity, we have *form* and *figure.*   These refer to the disposition of quantitative parts of a material body, as for example mathematical *figure* (triangular, circular, etc.) or the *form* (i.e., shape) of a vase in the concrete.

We can diagram all the above as follows:

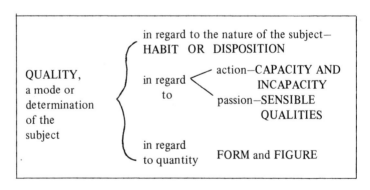

QUALITY, a mode or determination of the subject

- in regard to the nature of the subject— HABIT OR DISPOSITION
- in regard to
  - action—CAPACITY AND INCAPACITY
  - passion—SENSIBLE QUALITIES
- in regard to quantity — FORM and FIGURE

Truth, Man and God

It is basic to the philosophy of St. Thomas Aquinas that the human mind has a capacity to learn the truth of things from their qualities and activities, which are the objective characteristics of things. St. Augustine saw in this capacity of man a certain participation in the Divine Intelligence Itself. We can make the following parallel.

As St. Thomas found a starting point to God's existence in the absolute character of being and saw implied therein the actuality of the Absolute Being, so St. Augustine found the actuality of created truth (truth in our minds) as a sign of God as Absolute Truth. The mystery of human knowledge—as the mystery of being itself—can find no ultimate explanation except in God as the Regulating Source of Truth and Being. As philosophers have fallen into pantheism in contemplating being, as for example, Spinoza, so also some philosophers, viz., the Idealists, have made human truth the Absolute. A more apt solution to the mystery of knowledge lies in the thought of St. Augustine. In this connection, St. Thomas Aquinas interpreted the phrase of St. Augustine—"divine illumination in knowledge"—to mean that man's intellect itself is a "light" which comes from God. But, on the other hand, this "light" (or the human intellect) could not be brought from potency to act except under the influence of the First Cause, whose presence and activity is reasonably deducible from the fact of knowledge as well as from the operations of material things. To some modern philosophers, who are more impressed with the operations of the human mind than with those of the physical world, the emphasis of

St. Augustine might be a welcome insight. It might also be helpful in solving the riddles of Kant.

Augustine, Aquinas and Kant

In the philosophy of Kant there are three ideas, the Ego, the World and God, which do not fall under sensible experience and which, for Kant, are nevertheless innate in pure reason. Now, it is true that God as the Center of the World is implied in our knowledge of being as a totality, but is not immediately evident to the intellect. But, in the philosophy of Aquinas His presence can become evident. Also, God as the Implied Spirit in every conscious being is an unknown Presence, but in St. Augustine's philosophy this Presence is able to be reached by conscious reflection of the human soul upon itself. Finally, in the philosophy of both Saints, God is to be recognized as the Coordinator of both the *truth* of the *reality* of the world and the *reality* of *truth* in man's conscious knowledge of the world. Kant recognized a fact that he was unable to explain—the inevitable thrust of reason toward the knowledge of God in all knowledge of the world and toward the implication of another Ego in the very thought processes of man's mind, together with the prevailing insistence of human reason that neither the World nor the Ego is separable from the transcendent Being called God. Yet, according to St. Thomas, these conclusions are foreshadowed in man's natural knowledge of being and truth. "The beginning of all knowledge," he says (*Truth*, 18, 4) "consists in a certain confused knowledge of all things." Or, in another place (*Contra Gentiles,* I, 43): "Our intellect in understanding is extended to infinity."

Returning to the charts previously given on pages 55, 58, and 59, we should now contrast the categories of being in the accidental order, known through the senses, against the background of man's initial confused and general consciousness of being.

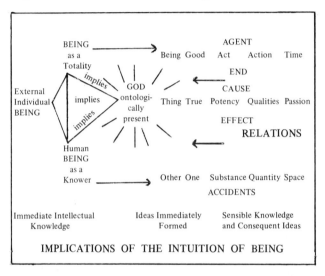

IMPLICATIONS OF THE INTUITION OF BEING

Unlike Kant, St. Thomas did not believe in innate ideas. But he did hold to certain natural concepts and principles which are naturally formed in man, and on which all future knowledge is based. The process of knowledge, for St. Thomas, is as it were, in a backward direction, going back to the most ontologically true and real in a gradual process from sense to an ever more vivid realization of the implications of the intellectual insight into being necessarily accompanying sense experience.

Comparison with Kant's innate categories and *a priori* sense intuitions and the three ideas of reason

WORLD
GOD
SOUL

The Three Ideas of REASON

MODALITY

Possibility
Existence
Necessity

Reality
Negation
Limitation

Unity
Plurality
Totality

Innate Categories

QUANTITY

Action
Reaction

Cause
QUALITY
Effect

Substance
Accident

RELATION

Time

Space

Sense Intuition

KANT'S INTUITIONS, CATEGORIES AND IDEAS

We can contrast the thought of the two thinkers by the following charts. The first shows the Kantian viewpoint, which should be studied in connection with the table above. The second chart shows the implications of human knowledge as taught by St. Thomas.

The consciousness of a self (subject) as simultaneous one (knower) and other (object known) is a mysterious fact, not to be explained, but accepted as absolute. For, this very fact must somehow reflect the Eternal, Immutable and Changeless Act (GOD) that no one will ever be able to fully comprehend.

In a word, I know that I am not outside reality (the other). Yet, in the act of knowledge, I know too that the reality as known (the other) is present also within me. Finally, I know *myself* as the inscrutable subject of my knowledge.

THE IMPLICATIONS OF HUMAN KNOWLEDGE

"However expert our knowledge about material things, there always remains a desire to know more.... Hence our restlessness and desire for more perfect knowledge.... Our natural desire, therefore, will not be quieted until we know the first cause...." (*Compendium Theologiae,* 104)

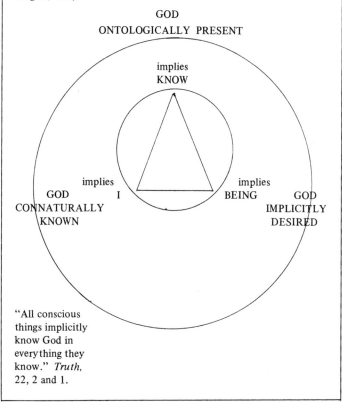

GOD
ONTOLOGICALLY PRESENT

implies
KNOW

implies
GOD   I
CONNATURALLY
KNOWN

implies
BEING   GOD
IMPLICITLY
DESIRED

"All conscious things implicitly know God in everything they know." *Truth,* 22, 2 and 1.

Concluding Comparison

It is interesting to note that one of the interpretations of St. Augustine's theory of illumination is the so-called regulatory theory, which holds that God's presence and co-operation in our thought processes constitutes a basic regulatory influence, which does not affect the content of our thought as such. Kant on his part attributes to the idea of *God* (as to the other two ideas of pure reason, *the self* and *the world*) a "regulative value." The human mind is so constituted that it naturally thinks of these objects, which contribute toward a unified and consistent interpretation of experience. For St. Augustine, the consciousness of the regulatory influence of these ideas is an indication of their objective validity. It seems that Kant had a vivid awareness of the former, while denying the latter. We may say that *St. Thomas* goes from the truth of being to the truth of mind to the truth of God. *St. Augustine* proceeds from the truth of mind (which springs from the truth of being) to the truth of God. *Kant,* keenly aware of the truth of mind, stops short refusing to plunge inwardly to the objectivity of self and reluctant either to step backward to the truth of being or to step forward to the truth of God. Thus, he seems to miss the depth, the width and the height of his own intuition.

8.

THE GOOD

"The good is what all things seek." These words of Aristotle tell us of a great drama enacted in the core of every being and in the totality of the universe at large. For all things act, and in acting they tend toward a good, toward a desirable end and toward their own perfection. This radical tendency in all things is called by Aristotle by the name of "entelechy" or "teleology." He considered this universal tendency in all things toward good an imitation of God, Whose supreme perfection is the cause of this inner drive for perfection in the whole universe. Christian philosophers and thinkers have taken up this thought. For St. Thomas, it is God's love that is the compelling driving force that gives existence to things and brings them to their end. Thus, goodness pervades all things. This happens because of God's Will. Since in creating all things, God shows His Will that they exist; they are desired by Him. In this relationship to His Will their goodness consists. He gives them all the perfections that they have, which make them desirable to themselves and possible ends of desire for other things. Thus every being—embodying in itself the sum total of perfections that it possesses—is *good,* i.e., desirable. As in the case of truth, the primary reference here is to God—in this case, to God's Will, Who desires

93

things to be and to be perfect according to their kind. Each thing is good absolutely, i.e., in itself, both existentially and essentially because (objectively) *it is good to be,* and to be according to one's kind or nature. It would not be good for a horse to be a cat, for then it would not be at all. Each thing is good also in relation to other things, because beings can be desirable to one another in many ways. The goodness of each thing finds expression in its activity, by which it seeks desirable perfections according to its nature. Its activity might also be of benefit to other things and become the term of desire of such things.

The Good as End

To understand the good, it is necessary to think of the good in terms of an *end.* The "end" of an action is the desired goal to be achieved by that action. An object of desire (i.e., a good) is the end toward which an appetite tends. The implication of "end" in every good is expressed in the scholastic formula: *Bonum habet rationem finis*—the good has the nature of an end.

Think of a concert, with its "grand finale" which the whole concert leads up to. Everything in the concert shares in the goodness (desirableness) of the end, inasmuch as it leads up to it. It is a useful *means* toward an *end.* The relationship to end is necessarily implied in every *useful* good. Finally, the enjoyment of the concert is related to the end, because the enjoyment is afforded only in achieving the end. Thus, the *pleasure-giving* good cannot be understood without taking into account the "end" or purpose of the act.

In relation to man, the goodness which is in all

things can be divided, following the pattern traced above, into the *befitting* (honorable) good, the *useful* good, and the *pleasure-giving* good. Man's befitting good is virtue, which is desirable *in itself* for man's perfection as man. Many other things may be *useful* goods (means toward some appropriate human ends). Finally, pleasure is an end which man often seeks, but from the nature of the case, every action which brings pleasure has some inherent purposefulness.

The Good as Analogous

In understanding goodness, attention should be paid to its analogous character. Of course, all the transcendentals are analogous, just as being itself. But it is especially in regard to goodness that varying degrees or grades of perfection stand out. It is *good* to exist even in the lowest realm of being. It is *better* to exist as a living being. And it is *best* to exist as an intelligent being and to act accordingly. In the words of St. Francis de Sales: the perfection of being is man; the perfection of man is spirit; the perfection of spirit is God; and the perfection of God is love. The final goodness of any being lies in its ultimate activity, and in the case of God, this is to love without measure, which follows upon His infinite intelligence and infinite, spiritual nature. This is in accord with the principle previously mentioned, *agere sequitur esse:* activity follows upon being in accordance with its nature and manifests what it is. Activity, and the end implied in activity, go hand in hand in the understanding of being as good.

In this context it is appropriate to interpret the words of St. Thomas: "All perfections pertain to the perfection of being." This, indeed, states that actuality is the most basic perfection. But the Saint is far from suggesting that within itself, being does not allow for varying degrees of perfection. In fact, all beings of limited perfection fall short of that enjoyed in the Being Wherein infinity of spirit is identified with infinity of intelligence and with the infinity of willingness, which is to love without measure. Goodness, like being, is proportionate to this Model. Only in God does the immanent activity of spirit terminate in Infinite Love with the consequence that, in this full sense, only God is good. In God alone is the diffusion of goodness infinite, in such a way that the term (end) of this diffusion is entirely within Himself without any dependence on outside reality.

Activity or Action in Creatures

All this, as well as the relationship to an end or purpose which is bound up with the concept of good, is sometimes expressed in the formula: *Bonum est diffusivum sui*—the good is diffusive of itself. The good attracts things to itself as to an end, a term of desire, in proportion to the diffusiveness of its activity, in which its own being terminates. In this sense, the axiom means the same as the preceding one—*bonum habet rationem finis* (the good has the nature of an end). There is another meaning of the expression, however, which without erasing the meaning just explained, brings out a different nuance in its significance. The good does good. The good produces good. Good is the natural product of the activity of anything good. This is in the realm of efficient causality and is very evident to us in the realm of created nature. Think of all the good things that nature can do. There is some good that is naturally intended in every action of nature—there is some good toward which the action tends. Here another formula is also used to express the same idea: there is purposefulness in every action; every action tends toward an end (good). Good is everywhere. Good is anything that exists. Good is the action which a being naturally performs, because this is the expression of its own powers of activity. Good is the result, the end, the purpose of the action performed. Everywhere the good; everywhere the performance of good; everywhere the achieving of some good—and all proceeding from the external diffusion of God's Infinite Goodness. Because He is all-good in Himself, He freely chose to spread His goodness abroad.

Evil

Yet, if all things are good, if all things tend toward the good, how is there evil in the world? Evil is the opposite, the absence of the good. Is it an illusion? A point of view? A purely relative term? For a portion of his life, St. Augustine, who had been a follower of the Manicheans, believed that evil was a supreme principle opposite to God and therefore something very real. But he later abandoned this position and set forth the teaching on this subject which has been accepted by Scholastic philosophy generally. Evil is not any positive reality, but a privation of reality—the lack of some perfection that a subject should have and is missing. This is not to say that evil is an illusion, but rather to insist that finite beings can be deprived of some of the goodness which belongs to them and which they ought to have. Such a privation, being the opposite of what is their good, is undesirable. It is unsuitable for them and renders them, as well, unsuitable for others. Evil, then, exists in some good, in the sense that some good thing is deprived of its goodness, but evil could not exist by itself as a separate reality. St. Augustine explains this well:

> Since the Author of all natures is supremely good, all natures are good; but because they are not, as their Author, supremely and unchangeably good, the good in them may be both decreased and diminished. But for good to be diminished is evil; although however much it be diminished, there must necessarily remain something (if it is still nature) whence it may be nature. (*Enchiridion,* xii).

In other words, if we were to deprive any nature of *all* its good absolutely, there would be *nothing* left. But as long as anything remains, there is a portion of good, notwithstanding the simultaneous privation of *some* due perfection. It is in this sense that we are to understand another axiom: *bonum ex integra causa, malum ex quolibet defectu.* We judge a thing's goodness by its completeness, according to whether it has everything it should have. But we may judge anything evil even for the least defect, if it lacks ever so little of the perfection that it should have.

Existentialism

Our line of reasoning in these pages does not follow nor agree with the thinking of a number of contemporary existentialists, who are atheists. This is not surprising. Our point of view, as that of St. Augustine, is from God's vantage point. All things desired by God are by that very fact good. Yet God does not interfere with the natural operations of His creatures. Physical evils in the world, where God allows the sometimes contradictory interests of secondary causes to take their course, are not desired for their own sakes, but for the good of the organization of the world as a whole. Similarly, God wills men to be free, with the consequent permission of evil effects flowing from some of the actions of men. Furthermore, He wills that intelligent men, by their own action and with His help, make this a better world. To understand all this we would have to know the final end that He has in view.

Obviously, for a person who does not believe in God, this reasoning does not make sense. Likewise, a person who does not believe in God may well reject the whole moral order willed by God. In such a case, a purely human law or individual caprice is substituted for the moral law, according to the "situation" of the individual man or of a given society.

But moral goodness, based on the understanding of God's Will, is absolutely essential for the attainment of man's goal, both as an individual and as a race. It pertains to the "good" of man as such, in accordance with all the principles about goodness explained in these pages and which have their proper application in the Philosophy of Morality.

All men naturally tend toward the "good" of man, set by God, in accordance with His intelligent and free nature. The frustration of God's plan for mankind in the world is the cause for the anguish of the whole of contemporary society. The awareness of the cause of this frustration can bring man to a greater maturity as he advances toward his destiny. For, in the words of St. Thomas:

> The first mover and author of the universe is Mind, and therefore its ultimate purpose is the good of Mind: and this is truth. *Contra Gentiles* I, 26.

9.

THE WONDROUS ENSEMBLE

No man can live in a vacuum. Neither can a philosopher do so. If he is interested in the ultimate explanation of the world in all its parts, and if he seeks to find the concepts and principles necessary for this task, he cannot shut his eyes to the *real* world in its global dimensions, in its vast expanding horizons, in its rapidly accelerating pace toward the future. He can separate philosophy neither from science nor theology, history nor life. Furthermore, the principles he has discovered in the "wonder of the real" should be elucidated on a global scale, so as to form a magnificent ensemble of Truth. We have spoken of the universality, not only of truth, but of unity and goodness as well.

But we live in a world where error competes with truth, evil with goodness, and both with a peaceful, harmonious and united world. How does this square with the abstract metaphysical principles which we have set forth in this book? How does the world, as we find it, relate to the fundamental philosophical questions raised in this book?

From the earliest times one of the most enticing problems of philosophy was *change.* Another great question concerned *"the one and the many."* *Evil* has always been an enigma for philosophers. Traditionally philosophy has always faced these questions and at least in some measure has sought to answer them with the principles outlined in this "basic sketch." It is now our task to try to apply them in a synthesis that is at once compatible with both the consciousness of modern man and the Christian world view.

Take "change." What is change, taken in a global sense, if not *evolution,* of which modern man is so conscious? Do the principles of *act* and *potency* apply in interpreting the evolutionary process? If so, how? Does evil, explained as a privation, make any sense in a world tormented by wars and violence? Do the seemingly increasing divisions among mankind promise any sort of *unity?*

The Christian Philosophy

Philosophy alone, understood in a strict sense, cannot answer these questions. But can philosophy be given a wider meaning? Is not philosophy a vision of the world, of man and of God, as presented by a great thinker, or thinkers? Taken in this sense, what philosophy, in fact, has been more influential than Christianity? How does Christian philosophy tie in its own view of the universe with the fundamental philosophical questions that we have considered?

The World as a Unit

We have seen how each thing of the substantial order presents itself as a distinct being and as a distinct unit. Yet these things are related to each other in manifold ways. The intelligent and provident direction of all things on a global scale requires the presence of God as immanent to the world at large. This means that the world receives its own consistency from the very presence of the Divine Being. We would expect that this immanent and regulating presence, necessary in the ontological order, be manifested on the physical, intellectual and moral orders. For God is one and the same Center of all these realms. Christians believe that God's immanence in the world has been manifested in a special way through history, in the Person of a Man named Jesus Christ. The following quotation of Cardinal Newman well expresses this belief:

> Christ's life brings together and concentrates truths concerning the chief good and law of our being, which wander idle and forlorn over the surface of the moral world and often appear to diverge from each other. It collects the scattered rays of light, which, in the first days of creation, were poured over the whole face of nature, into heaven, to rule over the day and the night, and to divide the light from darkness. Our Saviour has in Scripture all those abstract titles of moral excellence bestowed upon Him which philosophers have invented. He is the Word, the Light, the Life, the Truth, Wisdom, the Divine Glory. St. John announces it in the text: "The Life was manifested, and we have seen it." *University Sermons,* pp. 26-7.

The unity of the world with the Divine Principle is reflected as in a resplendent mirror in the souls of those who clearly understand that the World is a Whole, which is unified by the action and presence of the Infinite Divine Substance necessarily present to it. Such was the soul of Cardinal Newman, who saw the imprint of the Divine Face stamped on the Whole as well as on each part of the universe.   Furthermore, the great Englishman pointed out the reason for man's failure to see the unity of the world.   It is due to the blinding effect, global in magnitude, of the "dialectic of sin."

The Dialectic of Sin

The one world created by God was intended by Him to be a source of contact with Himself. This was how it was in the beginning of man's history, whose fulfillment in the various levels of existence (physical, intellectual and moral) was assured. God Himself was present to man's consciousness, and this presence was man's greatest gift and highest good.

But man chose to experience evil as well as good, and so deprived himself of the loving communication with God, Who had revealed Himself to man.   A new and tragic state ensued for man after his fall from this exalted condition of friendship with God.

Far different—explains Cardinal Newman—is our state since the fall:—at present our moral rectitude, such as it is, is acquired by trial, by discipline: but what does this really mean? By sinning, by suffering, by correcting ourselves, by improving. We advance to the truth by the experience of error; we succeed by failures. We know not how to do right except by having done wrong. We call virtue a mean—as considering it to lie between things that are wrong. We know what is right, not positively, but negatively;—we do not see the truth at once and make towards it, but we fall upon and try error, and find it *not* the truth. We grope about by touch, not by sight, and so by a miserable experience exhaust the possible modes of acting till nought is left, but truth remaining. Such is the process by which we proceed; we walk to heaven backward; we drive our arrows at a mark, and are the least. *Parochial and Plain Sermons,* N. Y., 1913, p. 103.

Seen in global perspective, the condition of man "walking to heaven backward" becomes the story of the advance of mankind through the centuries amid great difficulties and struggles. The control that man was to have had over that advance has been subjected to the continuing human decision to experience evil, but the over-all direction of man's advance is indicative of the unaltered plan of God for man's happiness. This is accomplished through Christ. In the words of Cardinal Newman:

Christ came. . .to gather together in one all the elements of good dispersed throughout the world, to make them His own, to illuminate them with Himself, to reform and refashion them into Himself. He came to make a new and better beginning of all things than Adam had been, and to be a fountain-head from which all good henceforth might flow. Hence it is said that "in the dispensation of the fullness of times" Almighty God "gathered together in one all things in Christ, both which are in heaven, and which are on earth." How He became a new commencement to things in heaven, we know not; nor know we adequately in what way

He recapitulated or ordered anew things on earth.
But this we know, that, the world being under the
dominion of Satan, and truth and goodness in it
being but as gems in the mine, or rather as metal
in the ore, He came to elicit, to disengage, to com-
bine, to purify, to perfect. And, further than this,
He came to new-create,—to begin a new line, and
construct a new kingdom on the earth: that what
had as yet laid in sin might become what it was at
first, and more than that. . . .He took on Him our
nature, that in God that nature might revive and
be restored; that it might be new born, and, after
being perfected on the Cross, might impart that
which itself was, as an incorruptible seed, for the
life of all who receive it in faith, till the end of
time. Hence He is called in Scripture the Beginning of the Creation of God, the First-begotten of
the dead, the First-fruits of the Resurrection.
Przywara, ed., *A Newman Synthesis*, (London,
1930), p. 159.

The End of Man

Beginning from a different starting point than Cardinal Newman, the Jesuit paleontologist of the Twentieth
Century, Pierre Teilhard de Chardin endeavored to relate
the early beginnings of mankind, as knowable to science,
to man's progress and ultimate destiny.

In his study of anthropology,[1] Teilhard thought that

---

1. See Pierre Teilhard de Chardin, *The Future of Man*, (N. Y., Harper
and Row, 1964); and *The Phenomenon of Man*, 1959. See also Francis
J. Klauder, *Aspects of the Thought of Teilhard de Chardin*, (North Quincy,
Mass., Christopher Publishing House, 1971).

he detected a pattern of development which he claimed is very indicative of the Future of Man. According to his principle of "complexity-consciousness" in biological evolution, there was an advance of ever more complex and ever more aware species of animals until Man appears as the first explicitly conscious being (he "knows that he knows"). Since man's appearance, however, there has been an advance (not along biological lines), but in social consciousness. The ultimate purpose of this direction, according to Teilhard, is a global consciousness of all mankind lovingly united as in one person. The only one capable of achieving this worldwide destiny, in the last analysis, is God, Who is its original Source (Alpha). And God, fulfilling this function is called Omega and has been manifested in Christ.

Here, we may say, we have a perfect application of the principles of act and potency on a universal scale. Man (*capax Dei*), capable in himself of being united with God, lost his original actualized condition of union with the Divine Substance. At the same time he stands in need of the actualization of many potentialities as a race. This is accomplished only within the framework of the dialectic of sin. And Christ is the One Center and Director both of man's restoration to God and of the development of the human race. He is the Way, the Truth and the Life, exercising His function in many ways and in different orders.

Incomparable Destiny

The principles governing the goodness of all things apply on a global as well as on an individual scale. The purpose of God's goodness in creating was to unite man-

kind with Himself. This comprehensive purpose lies
behind the motion of the universe and of man's history. This purpose shall not be defeated. Even though
God has permitted, and permits, a "great falling away"
from Himself, this is in accordance with man's decision
"to know evil" and his consequent "walking to heaven
backward." But the plan of God remains invincible.

Long ago St. Bonaventure compared history to a song,
whose succeeding parts lead up to the beautiful ending
ordained by God. And St. Augustine before him had
written in his immortal *City of God,* XI, XVIII:

> God would never have created a single angel—
> not even a single man—whose future wickedness
> He foresaw unless, at the same time, He knew of
> the good which would come of this evil. It was as
> though He meant the harmony of history, like the
> beauty of a poem, to be enriched by antithetical
> elements. . . .

Both these men knew that:

> . . .There will be one flock and one shepherd
> (John 10:16)
> . . .one body and one spirit, even as you were
> called in one hope of your calling; one Lord, one
> faith, one Baptism; one God and Father of all, Who
> is above all, and throughout all, and in us all
> (Ephesians 4:4-6).

God, Who is singing the song of creation, is distinct
from His song; and the song is distinct from Him, but
receives its beginning, continuance and its ending from
Him.

APPENDIX ONE: VARIOUS TABLES

TABLE ONE: Variation in Meaning of *Metaphysical,*
Physical, Moral and *Logical* as Applied to the
Transcendentals and Shown by Examples

Basic Meaning	Examples: Moral	Physical	Metaphysical	Logical
B E I N G Actuality	Free human acts	God, the Pure Act Actual spirits & matter	Possibles, which are ultimately ideas of God, the Pure Act	Ideas of things actually conceived by man's mind
I D E N T I T Y Changeless-ness (same-ness of a thing with itself)	Matter: identical in the common estimation of men	Spirit: subject to accidental change	God: unchange-able	any idea completely the same as another idea
U N I T Y Undivi-dedness	Human groups united in some purpose	Matter, not divided but divisible	God and all spirits: indivisible	a universal idea, with one (univocal) meaning
T R U T H Corres-pondence or rela-tionship to mind	Correspon-dence of human words with ideas	- - - - -	Correspon-dence of things with God's ideas	Correspon-dence of man's ideas with things
G O O D N E S S Desir-ability Relation-ship to will or appetite	Free human acts, as desired by God's Will and so understood by human reason	Desirable goods of the sensible order	Every being, desired by God and desirable for others	- - - - -

TABLE TWO: DISTINCTIONS

Difference of one thing (or concept) from another

Real:
exists
outside
the mind

Physical — between thing and thing

Metaphysical — between the principles of being

Mental:
exists only
in the mind

Major — two concepts, one of which is potentially contained in the other

Minor — two concepts, one of which actually implies the other

Verbal — two words for exactly the same thing

APPENDIX TWO: A LESSON FROM
EXISTENTIALISM AND PANTHEISM

Modern Existentialism can render us an important service. It reminds us that there is more to reality than our abstract conception of it. While we cannot go along with the Existentialists and deny value to abstract ideas, which represent essences, we can take a lesson from them in their emphasis on the *singularity* of each reality and of the actual interrelatednesses of all concrete things (*communion*), especially of all human beings.

This twofold insight of the Existentialists can at the same time usher us into the Divine Presence, by which God is immanent to all things. Hence all things (and especially human persons) can introduce (present) us to God.

The vivid sense of some Existentialists of singularity, communion and divine presence is nothing else than a connatural appreciation of the truths which traditionally have been expressed by the "analogy of being." Profiting by the light of Existentialism, we can come to a better grasp of ANALOGY, especially as applied to human persons. At the same time, perhaps we can get a deeper glance into reality as seen (in a confused way) by the Pantheists.

Seen in full perspective, each reality that stands before me (as, for instance, a fellow human being) embodies a "*nature*" that opens itself to the understanding and is clearly understood to be multipliable in other realities besides the singular one before me. This "nature" is represented (however inadequately, nevertheless truly) by the universal idea. At the same time I am struck by the individuality and singularity that each being presents, as well as by the *absoluteness* of the fact that *it exists.* The intuition of its existence (regardless of what the Existentialists may say) results in the marvelous, all-embracing, ever-varying IDEA OF BEING. But this rich and fecund idea, far from inducing me to get lost in useless abstractions in the mind, invites me back to the concrete being before me, to an ever more lucid understanding of *WHAT IS.* Here before me is the mystery of being carrying within it all the implications that are hidden from initial sight.

First, this being *IS,* yet it is not alone. Secondly, this reality is *similar* to its pars in the community of being; yet it is unique and set off from everything not itself. Thirdly, this thing is a sign of deeper realities than the senses can perceive. It not only indicates a nature which I can represent by some kind of an abstract idea. It indicates and is a sign of a Presence greater than itself which only reasoning can fully vindicate and which Faith confirms. It is a mysterious manifestation of Divine Presence, of a Divine Being superior (transcendent) to it and yet here present (immanent) supporting its radical contingency and preventing it from falling back into that nothingness which is at the heart of its own being. The Existentialists suggest that we concentrate on our own human person to come to a fuller realization of the contingency of one's own being and an awareness of a Divine Presence beyond the self.

Reason persuades me to conclude that this Divine Being (so weakly revealed, yet so ʋynamically present) is simultaneously *Something* and *Someone Distinct.* I can come to understand that this Something is a Subsisting Being, whose very nature is to exist, and Whose comprehension therefore escapes my understanding. At the same time, I understand that such a Being is *Someone Distinct* from every manifested thing. Everything that is, is related to this Divine Person, Who is God. The Self, or any other human person, or, for that matter, any individual thing that stands before me simultaneously reveals and hides Him. It is not so surprising that some philosophers have been confused by His presence and identified Him with the created manifestations of His Being. Of all the things that present themselves to us, the human person is most like the Divine Being and most likely to be confused with the Divine Reality. Thus, since the Pantheist considers total reality as divine, he naturally thinks of humanity as the highest expression of the divine reality. Yet Pantheism makes a great mistake when it extols "humanity" (an abstraction), whereas each human person, as *someone distinct,* is a closer approximation to the highest manifestation of divinity.

The Pantheist fails to see that the reality before us, as for instance, a fellow human being, while somewhat related to the divine being, is not itself divine. While it is to the credit of the Pantheist that he sees some relationship to the Divine in existing reality, he fails to see that this reality, though indeed related to divine being, is not related to the point of identification. If it were related to the point of identification, its very nature would be to exist. Now this is clearly not the case, as far as human reason can gauge. Together with the finite nature, the contingent singularity of each thing (so vividly understood by our contemporary Existentialists) clearly rules this out. What the Pantheist should seek to understand is that the very similarity of each thing to God would not be possible without a differentiating factor by which each thing (and especially human persons) is approximated to God, and each to a definite degree. Thus, the relationship that each thing has to God, Who is present to it, falls short of identifying with Him. Yet this relationship is at the core and center of its being. And no being can be understood unless as related to Him, and related therefore to every other thing related to Him. Being, then, comes out to mean the distinctive relationship that each thing holds in the community of being, which all falls short of the fullness of Being; this pertains alone to that Someone Hidden Who is yet revealed by all created things because of their relationship to Him.

This, then, is the final word of all philosophy that the World is a Whole at whose Center is God; and all beings are at once His relatives, and relatives to each other. But to *know* this is not enough: it is an end, a goal, an achievement *to be realized.* And, as a contemporary philosopher has said, when the world arrives at this final destination and mankind turns all its energies of love to harness the universe for God, then Man will have discovered for a second time *fire!*